FAITH AND BELIEVING

A Theological Distinction

Dr. Maxwell Shimba

Printed by Shimba Publishing LLC
Printed in the United States of America

TABLE OF CONTENTS

INTRODUCTION

Faith and believing are foundational to the Christian journey, and while they are often used interchangeably, they carry distinct theological meanings that are essential to understanding a life lived in relationship with God. To "believe" is generally understood as accepting something to be true. However, in the Bible, "faith" goes beyond mere intellectual acknowledgment; it involves trusting, relying, and committing oneself wholly to God. In this sense, faith is not just a state of mind but an active engagement of the heart and will with God's purposes.

The Bible places immense emphasis on faith as the cornerstone of a life that pleases God. Hebrews 11:6 states, "And without faith it is impossible to please God, because anyone who comes to him must believe that he exists and that he rewards those who earnestly seek him." This verse highlights two critical elements: belief in God's existence and a trust in His goodness. Faith, therefore, is more than a mental affirmation; it requires a deep, relational trust in God's nature, promises, and intentions toward us.

The Nature of Belief

Belief is often the starting point for anyone's journey with God. In a Christian context, belief is the acknowledgment of God's truth: accepting His existence, His word, and His power as absolute. John 3:16 is one of the most cited verses to underscore belief's importance, stating that "whoever believes in Him shall not perish but have eternal life." Belief here signifies a fundamental acceptance of Jesus Christ as Savior and the foundation of salvation. However, belief alone, while necessary, does not encompass the fullness of what God desires for us.

The apostle James addresses this in his letter, reminding readers that even demons "believe" in God and "shudder" (James 2:19). Thus, belief by itself, without trust and commitment, is incomplete in the biblical view. True belief should ideally lead to faith, a trust that moves beyond acknowledgment to transformation and action.

The Depth and Power of Faith

Faith, in its essence, involves a surrender to God's character, wisdom, and plans. Hebrews 11:1 defines faith as "the substance of things hoped for, the evidence of things not seen." This verse presents faith as the unseen reality of a believer's life; it is something tangible, albeit not visible to the eye. Faith is thus a conviction that God's promises are trustworthy, even when their fulfillment is yet to come.

The lives of biblical figures like Abraham, Moses, and David exemplify faith's depth. Abraham's willingness to leave his homeland or offer his son Isaac as a sacrifice shows a faith that went beyond mere belief in God's words; it reflected an active trust in God's character and promises. Faith becomes an active, transformational force, where belief is put into practice through obedience, action, and perseverance.

Why Faith is Essential to Pleasing God

The Bible emphasizes that without faith, it is impossible to please God (Hebrews 11:6). This profound statement reveals the nature of our relationship with God, one that is based not on human achievement or intellectual understanding alone but on trust. Here are several reasons why faith is so central to a life that honors God:

1. Faith Reflects Reliance on God's Character: When we have faith, we recognize that God is who He says He is—faithful, good, and sovereign. By trusting in His nature and promises, we are essentially acknowledging that He is worthy of our devotion, which is deeply pleasing to Him.

2. Faith Invites God into Our Lives: Faith is a form of humility that says, "I cannot do this alone; I need You, God." This posture invites God to work in and through us. Scripture shows that God's power often flows through those who exhibit trust in Him. For example, Jesus often told those He

healed, "Your faith has made you well" (Matthew 9:22), showing that faith actively allows God's will to unfold in our lives.

3. Faith Is a Response to God's Revelation: Throughout Scripture, God reveals Himself and His will to His people. Faith is our response to that revelation. By trusting what God has revealed—even when it is not visible or fully understood—we affirm that God's wisdom is higher than our own, which aligns us with His purposes.

4. Faith Results in Obedience and Transformation: Faith is transformative. It doesn't merely accept God's truth intellectually but allows that truth to change how we live. True faith leads to a life of obedience and moral alignment with God's word. James 2:26 tells us, "faith without works is dead," underscoring that faith should lead to actions that reflect God's love and holiness.

Faith and Believing in Today's World

In a world that increasingly values tangible proof and rational understanding, faith can sometimes feel countercultural or difficult to grasp. Belief is often considered credible if it aligns with scientific or logical frameworks. But faith calls us to trust beyond what we can verify empirically, requiring us to rely on a relational understanding of God. This is not a blind trust; rather, it is rooted in the history, promises, and character of a faithful God. Faith asks us to see reality through the lens of God's word, trusting that He is working even when His actions aren't immediately visible.

Moving from Belief to Faith

The journey from belief to faith is essential for deepening one's spiritual life. Belief provides the foundational acknowledgment of God's reality, but faith brings this belief into every aspect of life, guiding decisions, actions, and attitudes. While belief may begin with accepting that God exists, faith develops as one actively places their trust in God's presence, power, and goodness. Faith encompasses a relationship with God that allows Him to guide, comfort, and empower His people, leading to a life that mirrors His love, justice, and mercy.

This book seeks to explore this theological distinction between faith and believing, not only to clarify these concepts but to deepen our understanding and practice of each. Throughout the following chapters, we will delve into the ways faith and belief interact, how they appear in the Bible, and how they shape our spiritual lives. By examining faith as both gift and response, we will see why it is essential for living a life that pleases God and for developing a lasting, dynamic relationship with Him.

The question of whether faith is more important than believing invites a deeper look into their roles in the Christian life. Both faith and belief are crucial, yet they function differently. Believing is foundational; it's the starting point for understanding and accepting God's truth. Faith, however, builds upon belief, moving from intellectual acceptance to a lived relationship of trust, reliance, and commitment to God. In this way, faith can be seen as both a culmination and an elevation of belief—an essential step for those who seek not just to acknowledge God's existence but to experience a transformed life in relationship with Him.

Belief is a necessary beginning. For example, John 3:16 states that "whoever believes in Him shall not perish but have eternal life." Belief in Jesus Christ as Savior and acceptance of the gospel is the foundation of salvation. It is the first response of a person who hears and accepts the truth about God. However, belief alone can remain static if it is not accompanied by a deeper commitment. The Bible illustrates that even demons "believe" in God and recognize His power (James 2:19), yet they do not live in alignment with God's will, nor do they trust Him. Thus, belief alone, without faith, lacks the trust and surrender that true discipleship requires.

Faith is the dynamic outgrowth of belief; it engages our entire being and transforms belief into a sustained, trusting relationship with God. Hebrews 11:1 defines faith as "the substance of things hoped for, the evidence of things not seen." Faith involves commitment, action, and a willingness to trust in God's promises, even when those promises are unseen. It requires a step beyond intellectual assent into trust and action. Faith compels a person to rely on God's wisdom over their own, to walk in obedience even when outcomes are uncertain, and to live in alignment with God's purposes.

An illustration of this dynamic relationship is seen in Abraham's story. Abraham believed in God's promise that he would be the father of many nations, yet it was his faith—demonstrated by his willingness to leave his homeland and even to sacrifice his son Isaac—that marked him as "righteous" in God's eyes (Romans 4:3). His belief in God's word laid the groundwork, but his faith—evidenced through actions of trust and obedience—fulfilled it.

Thus, while belief is essential, faith is indispensable for a life that truly pleases God. Faith takes belief and activates it, transforming it into a life lived in active relationship with God. In this sense, faith can be understood as both a greater and more mature expression of belief. Belief acknowledges that God exists; faith allows one to entrust their life to Him, walking daily in His promises.

In summary, both faith and belief are critical, but faith represents a deeper commitment that moves beyond acknowledgment to transformation. Without belief, faith would have no foundation; without faith, belief would lack the power to change lives and fulfill God's purpose. Thus, faith, built on belief, is ultimately what God seeks from His followers—a living trust that shapes our lives and draws us closer to Him.

DR. MAXWELL SHIMBA

CHAPTER 01

INTRODUCTION TO FAITH AND BELIEVING

In the Christian journey, we frequently hear the terms "faith" and "believing" used interchangeably, as though they are synonymous. While these two concepts are deeply connected, they represent different aspects of our relationship with God. Grasping the theological distinction between faith and believing is essential for anyone seeking to deepen their walk with God. In this chapter, we will delve into what it means to believe, what it means to have faith, and how these two elements work together in a Christian's spiritual life.

Believing, in its simplest form, is the acceptance of truth. It involves acknowledging that something is real or valid, usually based on evidence or conviction. However, faith goes beyond intellectual agreement. Faith involves trust, commitment, and reliance on God. It is the foundation of the Christian life, empowering us to act, live, and endure in ways that mere belief cannot. Together, faith and believing shape our relationship with God, but it is crucial to understand the theological nuances that distinguish them.

Biblical Definitions of Faith and Believing

The Bible offers clear insights into both faith and believing. In the New Testament, two Greek words primarily define these concepts. The Greek word for belief is pisteuo, which means to believe, to trust, or to have confidence in something or someone. The Greek word for faith is pistis, which refers to trust or firm persuasion, particularly in God or Christ.

John 3:16 gives us a foundational view of belief:

"For God so loved the world that He gave His one and only Son, that whoever believes in Him shall not perish but have eternal life."

Here, belief is presented as the necessary step for receiving eternal life. To believe in Jesus means to trust in the truth of who He is and the salvation He offers. But while this belief is essential, the Bible also clarifies that belief alone does not constitute a complete Christian life.

In contrast, Hebrews 11:1 provides a definition of faith:

"Now faith is the substance of things hoped for, the evidence of things not seen."

Faith is portrayed as a conviction, a deep assurance that transcends visible evidence. It involves placing one's trust not just in the truth but in the trustworthiness of God. Faith includes an element of belief, but it extends far beyond it—it empowers us to live according to God's promises, even when those promises are not yet fulfilled.

Belief as the Foundation

Believing is often the first step toward faith. It is the intellectual and emotional acceptance that the gospel is true. Romans 10:9 emphasizes the importance of belief in salvation:

"If you declare with your mouth, 'Jesus is Lord,' and believe in your heart that God raised him from the dead, you will be saved."

Belief here is more than a mental acknowledgment; it is a conviction that Jesus is Lord and that He is worthy of trust. This belief serves as the foundation of salvation, but it does not stand alone. For belief to be transformative, it must move us toward a deeper trust in God—this is where faith comes into play.

The apostle James presents a warning about belief without action:

_"You believe that there is one God. Good! Even the demons believe that—and shudder." (James 2:19)

Here, James addresses the danger of mere intellectual belief without faith. The demons believe in God—they know of His existence and power—yet they lack the faith that leads to submission and transformation. This passage illustrates that belief, while necessary, is not sufficient for a living, dynamic relationship with God. It must be accompanied by faith.

Faith as Trust and Reliance

Faith, on the other hand, is not just the acceptance of facts; it is trust in the unseen and unknown, and reliance on God's character. Hebrews 11 provides a powerful list of people who acted out of faith, despite not always seeing the fulfillment of God's promises during their lifetime. For example, Hebrews 11:8 speaks of Abraham:

"By faith Abraham obeyed when he was called to go out to the place which he would receive as an inheritance. And he went out, not knowing where he was going."

Abraham did not merely believe that God existed; he trusted God enough to leave his home and journey to an unknown land. His faith moved beyond intellectual belief into action and obedience. This is the essence of faith: it is trust that compels us to act on what we believe.

Faith, in its full expression, requires commitment. In James 2:17, the Bible says,

"Faith by itself, if it is not accompanied by action, is dead."

Faith produces a change in behavior—it results in works that demonstrate trust in God. This is why faith is often described as living, whereas mere belief can be static. Faith involves stepping out, trusting in God's promises even when the outcome is uncertain.

The Relationship Between Faith and Believing

Belief is essential to faith, but faith cannot be reduced to mere belief. Faith is belief in action. It is what happens when belief is combined with trust, reliance, and commitment to God. John 20:27-29 provides a clear example of this relationship through the story of Thomas. After the resurrection, Thomas struggled to believe in Jesus' resurrection until he saw the physical evidence. Jesus said to him,

"Because you have seen me, you have believed; blessed are those who have not seen and yet have believed."

Here, we see the distinction between believing based on evidence and having faith in the absence of visible proof. Faith transcends the need for physical evidence; it is based on trust in God's character and promises.

This relationship is further explained in Ephesians 2:8-9, where Paul writes:

"For by grace you have been saved through faith, and that not of yourselves; it is the gift of God, not of works, lest anyone should boast."

Faith is a gift of grace. It is not something we generate on our own, but something that God imparts to us. While believing involves our intellectual response to the gospel, faith is God's gift that empowers us to trust and live according to that belief.

Believing and faith are distinct but intertwined concepts in the Christian life. Believing involves accepting the truth of God's word and acknowledging the reality of Christ's life, death, and resurrection. Faith, however, takes that belief and translates it into trust, action, and reliance on God's promises. Without belief, faith cannot begin, but without faith, belief is incomplete.

As we explore these theological distinctions in greater depth throughout this book, we will see that both believing and faith are essential to a life that pleases God. Believing is the foundation, but faith is the structure that shapes and supports a fulfilling, transformative relationship with God. Understanding this distinction is not only crucial to our theology but also to our daily walk with God, as we learn to trust Him more deeply with every step.

Expository Bible Study and Commentary with Strong's Concordance on Faith and Believing

In exploring the theological and practical distinctions between "faith" and "believing," we'll look at several key Bible verses that ground these concepts in scripture. Through this, we'll utilize Strong's Concordance to unpack the original Greek and Hebrew meanings and gain a deeper understanding of how faith and believing operate within the life of a Christian.

Key Terms in Strong's Concordance:

1. Faith (πίστις, pistis) - Strong's G4102

2. Believe (πιστεύω, pisteuo) - Strong's G4100

3. Trust (בָּטַח, batach) - Strong's H982 (Old Testament context)

Expository Bible Study and Commentary

Hebrews 11:1 - Defining Faith

"Now faith (pistis - G4102) is the substance of things hoped for, the evidence of things not seen."

- Strong's Analysis: "Pistis" (G4102) refers to a conviction or assurance, specifically a firm trust in God and His promises.

- Commentary: Hebrews 11:1 provides one of the most well-known definitions of faith in scripture, emphasizing its nature as an assurance of things not yet visible. Here, faith moves beyond intellectual agreement to become an active conviction. It implies a trust in God's promises, even when the fulfillment is unseen. Faith acts as a bridge between hope and reality, transforming an abstract belief in God's promises into a confident assurance that influences one's actions and mindset.

John 3:16 - The Beginning of Belief

"For God so loved the world that He gave His only begotten Son, that whoever believes (pisteuo - G4100) in Him should not perish but have everlasting life."

- Strong's Analysis: "Pisteuo" (G4100) implies an acceptance of truth, often translated as "to have faith in" or "to entrust."

- Commentary: In John 3:16, "believing" (pisteuo) denotes an initial, necessary act of accepting the gospel truth. This verse underlines that believing is foundational; it is the starting point where a person acknowledges the truth of Jesus Christ and accepts the offer of salvation. Yet belief here is still limited to mental assent unless it progresses to faith—a deeper relational trust in Jesus that translates into a transformed life.

James 2:19 - Faith versus Intellectual Belief

"You believe that there is one God. Good! Even the demons believe (pisteuo - G4100) — and shudder."

- Strong's Analysis: Here, "pisteuo" again represents intellectual assent or recognition of fact.

- Commentary: James provides a cautionary view of "belief" alone, illustrating that merely acknowledging God's existence doesn't equate to saving faith. Even demons "believe" that God exists, but this belief lacks a relational component with God. True faith, by contrast, goes beyond intellectual belief; it includes trust, surrender, and a willingness to live according to God's will.

Romans 10:9 - Belief and Confession

"If you declare with your mouth, 'Jesus is Lord,' and believe (pisteuo - G4100) in your heart that God raised him from the dead, you will be saved."

- Strong's Analysis: "Pisteuo" in this context points to a belief that goes beyond the intellect, engaging the heart.

- Commentary: Romans 10:9 suggests that belief is not merely cognitive; it's a heartfelt conviction. This belief in the resurrection, accompanied by confession, brings about salvation. Yet, it hints at the beginning of faith, as belief in the heart leads a person toward a life that is fully entrusted to Jesus, growing into active faith.

Genesis 15:6 - Faith as Righteousness

"Abram believed (batach - H982) the LORD, and he credited it to him as righteousness."

- Strong's Analysis: "Batach" (H982) in Hebrew refers to trusting or placing confidence in.

- Commentary: This Old Testament passage illustrates the trust aspect of faith. Abram's belief in God wasn't simply an acceptance of information; it was a deep trust in God's promises, despite his circumstances. God honored this faith by counting it as righteousness, revealing that faith goes beyond intellectual belief to engage our trust and loyalty to God.

Hebrews 11:6 - Pleasing God through Faith

"And without faith (pistis - G4102), it is impossible to please God, because anyone who comes to him must believe (pisteuo - G4100) that he exists and that he rewards those who earnestly seek him."

- Strong's Analysis: "Pistis" and "Pisteuo" both appear, distinguishing between believing in God's existence and having a relationship grounded in faith.

- Commentary: Hebrews 11:6 clearly separates "believing" in God's existence from the faith that pleases Him. It stresses that to truly please God, a person's belief must evolve into faith—a relationship of trust and commitment. Faith involves active seeking, reflecting a life that earnestly seeks alignment with God's will.

Applying the Exposition

1. Belief as the Foundation: In the Christian life, believing serves as the essential beginning, the point at which an individual assents to the truth about God and His works. Without believing, faith has no foundation.

2. Faith as Relationship and Action: Faith moves belief into the realm of lived experience. Hebrews 11 shows us that faith results in action—whether in obedience, as with Abraham, or courage, as with Moses. Faith, therefore, is a relational response to God, grounded in trust and characterized by action.

3. Why Faith Pleases God: Faith pleases God because it reflects a life fully entrusted to Him, one that mirrors His own nature of love, commitment, and faithfulness. Belief recognizes God's existence, but faith invites Him into every part of our lives.

In this study of faith and believing, we see that both are essential elements of the Christian journey. Believing is where we start—acknowledging God's truths and accepting His invitation. Faith, however, is where we grow, transforming belief into trust and relational depth with God. Through the lens of Strong's Concordance, we understand that these terms, though interconnected, reflect different stages of the spiritual life. Belief is the intellectual seed; faith is the trust-filled tree that produces spiritual fruit. Thus, both are indispensable but serve unique purposes in the life of a believer.

DEFINING FAITH: THE HEART OF CHRISTIAN THEOLOGY

Faith is one of the central themes of Christian theology, and it permeates every aspect of the believer's life. Theologically, faith is far more than simply believing certain facts about God; it is a holistic response to God's revelation that engages the heart, mind, and will. It moves beyond intellectual assent and involves trust, fidelity, and action. The Greek word for faith, pistis, conveys this depth—it means trust, loyalty, and commitment to someone or something.

Faith is crucial because it connects us to God in a way that nothing else can. It bridges the gap between our finite understanding and God's infinite wisdom, allowing us to trust Him even when we cannot see or comprehend His plans. This chapter will delve into the biblical definition of faith, explain why God loves people of faith, and demonstrate the importance of faith in believing and trusting in God.

The Biblical Definition of Faith

The Bible presents faith as the cornerstone of the Christian life. One of the most well-known and profound definitions of faith is found in Hebrews 11:1, where the writer states:

"Now faith is the substance of things hoped for, the evidence of things not seen."

This verse reveals that faith is both a tangible substance and a form of evidence. Faith gives substance to our hope—it brings the promises of God into the present moment, even before they are fully realized. It is the foundation upon which believers stand, enabling them to hold fast to God's promises even when they are not immediately visible.

Faith is not blind; it is based on the trustworthiness of God, who has revealed Himself throughout history and in His Word. Although the fulfillment of God's promises may not always be visible to the human eye, faith allows believers to live as though those promises are already a reality. This is why Romans 4:20-21 speaks of Abraham's faith:

"Yet he did not waver through unbelief regarding the promise of God, but was strengthened in his faith and gave glory to God, being fully persuaded that God had power to do what he had promised."

Abraham's faith was not merely belief in God's existence but trust in His character and His ability to fulfill His promises. His faith was grounded in the assurance that God was faithful and able to perform what He had promised, even when circumstances seemed to contradict it.

Faith as a Response to God's Revelation

Faith, from a theological perspective, is a response to God's revelation. It is not something that originates in us but is initiated by God. In Romans 10:17, Paul writes:

"So then faith comes by hearing, and hearing by the word of God."

Faith arises when we hear and respond to the Word of God. God's self-revelation—whether through Scripture, the life of Jesus Christ, or the prompting of the Holy Spirit—calls us to trust Him. Faith is not merely the result of human reasoning but is stirred by the truth of God's Word and His promises. When God speaks, faith is the proper response to His voice.

This connection between revelation and faith is why faith is described as a gift from God. In Ephesians 2:8, Paul says:

_"For by grace you have been saved through faith, and that not of yourselves; it is the gift of God."

This means that faith is not something we produce on our own. God, in His grace, enables us to believe and trust in Him. This is why faith is considered both a human act and a divine gift—it requires our response, but it is God who initiates and empowers that response.

Why God Loves People of Faith

God loves people of faith because faith reflects a profound trust in His character and His promises. Faith acknowledges God's sovereignty, wisdom, and goodness, even when circumstances challenge our understanding. Hebrews 11:6 makes it clear how essential faith is in our relationship with God:

"And without faith it is impossible to please God, because anyone who comes to him must believe that he exists and that he rewards those who earnestly seek him."

God is pleased by faith because it demonstrates reliance on Him, rather than on human strength or understanding. Faith is the acknowledgment that, despite our limitations, God is trustworthy and capable of fulfilling His purposes. When we live by faith, we show that we are confident in God's plan, timing, and provision, even when life is difficult or unclear.

An excellent example of God's love for people of faith is found in the story of the centurion in Matthew 8:5-13. The centurion asked Jesus to heal his servant, demonstrating his faith by saying:

_"Lord, I do not deserve to have you come under my roof. But just say the word, and my servant will be healed." (Matthew 8:8)

Jesus marveled at his faith, stating:

_"Truly I tell you, I have not found anyone in Israel with such great faith." (Matthew 8:10)

The centurion's faith pleased Jesus because it reflected total confidence in Jesus' authority. He trusted that Jesus' power transcended physical presence, and his faith resulted in his servant's healing. God loves such faith because it honors His power and trustworthiness.

The Importance of Faith in Believing God

Faith is essential in believing in God because it moves belief from mere intellectual assent to a trust that transforms how we live. James 2:17 tells us that:

"Faith by itself, if it does not have works, is dead."

In this context, James is not arguing that works earn salvation but rather that true faith is evidenced by action. Faith that does not lead to trust and obedience is not genuine faith. Believing that God exists is foundational, but faith requires that we live in accordance with that belief. In other words, belief is the starting point, but faith is what propels belief into action.

Consider the example of Noah in Hebrews 11:7:

"By faith Noah, when warned about things not yet seen, in holy fear built an ark to save his family. By his faith he condemned the world and became heir of the righteousness that is in keeping with faith."

Noah's faith moved him to action. He believed God's warning about the flood and demonstrated his faith by building the ark, even though it had never rained in such a way before. His belief in God's word led to trust and obedience, which is the hallmark of faith. This example illustrates that faith is not static; it is dynamic and responsive to God's commands.

Faith is also critical because it sustains us through trials. 1 Peter 1:6-7 explains:

"In all this you greatly rejoice, though now for a little while you may have had to suffer grief in all kinds of trials. These have come so that the proven genuineness of your faith—of greater worth than gold, which perishes even though refined by fire—may result in praise, glory and honor when Jesus Christ is revealed."

Faith is the means by which believers endure suffering, trusting that God's purposes are being fulfilled even in hardship. It is through faith that we navigate life's difficulties, secure in the knowledge that God is with us and will ultimately redeem every situation.

Faith as the Heart of Believing

Faith is the heart of believing in God because it moves beyond intellectual acknowledgment into a transformative relationship with Him. It requires trust, action, and fidelity to God's promises. The Bible consistently teaches that faith is not merely believing that God exists but believing in God—trusting His character, His word, and His promises.

Faith is the vehicle by which we enter into salvation, live out our daily Christian walk, and endure trials with confidence in God's provision and plan. As 2 Corinthians 5:7 reminds us:

"For we walk by faith, not by sight."

Faith enables us to live beyond the limitations of human sight and understanding, grounded in the certainty of God's truth. It is this deep and abiding trust in God that pleases Him and defines the Christian life. Without faith, we cannot truly believe in the fullness of who God is or experience the richness of His promises.

Expository Bible Study and Commentary with Strong's Concordance: Faith as a

Fundamental Theological Foundation in Christian Belief

Chapter 2 examines faith not only as a concept but as a fundamental theological foundation in Christian belief. Faith is essential for salvation, spiritual growth, and maintaining a relationship with God. Using Strong's Concordance, we'll explore faith in its Greek and Hebrew meanings, examining passages that reveal its theological depth and significance.

Key Terms in Strong's Concordance:

1. Faith (πίστις, pistis) - Strong's G4102

2. Hope (ἐλπίς, elpis) - Strong's G1680

3. Trust (בָּטַח, batach) - Strong's H982 (Old Testament)

4. Assurance (ὑπόστασις, hypostasis) - Strong's G5287

Expository Bible Study and Commentary

Hebrews 11:1 - Faith as Substance and Evidence

"Now faith (pistis - G4102) is the substance of things hoped for, the evidence of things not seen."

- Strong's Analysis: "Pistis" (G4102) in Greek signifies conviction, reliance upon Christ for salvation, and assurance.

- Commentary: Hebrews 11:1 is often cited as a foundational verse for understanding the nature of faith. Here, faith is described as both "substance" (hypostasis - G5287) and "evidence." The term "substance" or "hypostasis" suggests an underlying reality or assurance that gives foundation to what we hope for in God. Faith, therefore, is not a blind leap but a confident assurance, a divine persuasion that anchors believers in the unseen promises of God.

Romans 10:17 - Faith Comes by Hearing

"So then faith (pistis - G4102) comes by hearing, and hearing by the word of God."

- Strong's Analysis: "Pistis" here reflects trust that originates from being convinced by divine truth.

- Commentary: This verse links faith directly to the Word of God, illustrating that faith is generated not by human initiative but by hearing and internalizing God's promises. Theologically, this speaks to the transformative power of Scripture, as the Word functions as the source and sustenance of faith. By hearing God's Word, individuals come into contact with divine truth, enabling faith to take root as an active, living conviction.

Ephesians 2:8-9 - Faith as a Gift of Grace

"For by grace you have been saved through faith (pistis - G4102), and that not of yourselves; it is the gift of God, not of works, lest anyone should boast."

- Strong's Analysis: Here, "pistis" underlines faith as both reliance on God and a divine gift, implying that faith itself is not humanly generated but divinely bestowed.

- Commentary: In Ephesians 2:8-9, Paul emphasizes that faith is not a work or a merit-based accomplishment but a gift of God's grace. The theological implication is profound: faith is not something we can achieve by our own efforts. Instead, it is a gracious act of God, transforming believers and enabling them to respond to His offer of salvation. This passage highlights the humility required in faith, as it points back to God as the source, thus removing any grounds for human boasting.

Galatians 2:20 - Faith in the Life of the Believer

"I have been crucified with Christ; it is no longer I who live, but Christ lives in me; and the life which I now live in the flesh I live by faith (pistis - G4102) in the Son of God, who loved me and gave Himself for me."

- Strong's Analysis: "Pistis" here encompasses a faith that transforms life, aligning the believer's life with Christ's own.

- Commentary: In this verse, Paul portrays faith as the means through which believers experience a new life in

Christ. Faith here is transformative, guiding the Christian to a self-denial that is not just intellectual but involves every aspect of one's being. Theologically, this reflects the concept of union with Christ, whereby faith unites the believer to Christ's death and resurrection, resulting in a life that is empowered and directed by His Spirit. It's a daily living faith that alters actions, motivations, and identity.

James 2:17 - Faith and Works

"Thus also faith (pistis - G4102) by itself, if it does not have works, is dead."

- Strong's Analysis: Here, "pistis" indicates an active and productive trust in God that naturally results in works.

- Commentary: James challenges a passive or purely intellectual understanding of faith, asserting that genuine faith is inherently active. Faith, according to James, must produce tangible outcomes, such as good works, to be considered living and authentic. Theologically, this verse points to the fruit-bearing nature of true faith—it cannot remain idle but instead inspires actions that reflect the love, justice, and mercy of God. James' assertion reinforces that faith without transformation of behavior is incomplete and lifeless.

Proverbs 3:5 - Trust in the Old Testament Perspective

"Trust (batach - H982) in the LORD with all your heart, and lean not on your own understanding."

- Strong's Analysis: "Batach" in Hebrew is to have confidence or trust, often denoting a reliance on God's character and promises.

- Commentary: In the Old Testament, trust (batach) closely parallels the New Testament concept of faith. Trust here reflects an unwavering dependence on God, rooted in a relationship with Him. This verse underscores that genuine faith involves forsaking one's own understanding and relying wholly on God. Theologically, it introduces the Old Testament view of faith as a life orientation that prioritizes God's wisdom and guidance above all else.

Theological Reflections on Faith

1. Faith as Divine Persuasion: Faith, in its essence, is the "substance" or foundation of the Christian life. It's a divine persuasion that comes from encountering God's character and His promises through His Word. This aligns believers' hearts and minds to a reality grounded in divine truth rather than mere human reasoning.

2. Faith and Salvation: As Ephesians 2:8-9 emphasizes, salvation by faith is a gift from God, which both humbles the believer and glorifies God as the source of faith. Faith is thus the means by which God's grace is received, providing salvation and leading to spiritual transformation.

3. Active Faith and Transformation: Faith is not static; rather, it's dynamic and life-changing. James 2:17 and Galatians 2:20 both stress that faith must produce change, guiding actions that reflect God's will and purpose. Faith is not merely belief in God's existence but a daily trust in His plans and promises.

4. Old and New Testament Continuity: The concept of trust in God found in Proverbs (batach) mirrors the New Testament's understanding of faith as trust. This continuity between the Testaments demonstrates that faith has always been about complete reliance on God's character, wisdom, and sovereignty.

Faith, according to theological tradition and biblical evidence, encompasses more than a mental acknowledgment of God's existence; it's an act of total surrender and dependence on God. By using Strong's Concordance, we see faith as a divinely inspired conviction (pistis) that leads to both assurance and action. It is by this faith that Christians live, are transformed, and, ultimately, please God. The Christian life, therefore, is marked by a growing, enduring faith that permeates every thought, decision, and action, grounded in the assurance of God's presence and promises.

CHAPTER 03

BELIEVING: THE STARTING POINT

Believing is where the journey toward faith begins. It is the first step in acknowledging the truth of God, His word, and the reality of the gospel message. In the Bible, believing is portrayed as essential for salvation and as the foundation upon which faith is built. However, while belief is critical, it is not the end goal of the Christian journey. Believing leads to something much deeper—faith, which transforms belief into a lived trust and reliance on God.

Theological reflection on belief demonstrates that while belief is necessary, it is insufficient on its own. Belief can remain an intellectual acknowledgment of facts, but when it is paired with faith, it becomes transformative. In this chapter, we will explore the nature of belief in the Bible, how it serves as the starting point of faith, and why belief alone is not enough for a dynamic relationship with God.

The Nature of Belief in the Bible

Belief is the cognitive act of accepting something as true. In a Christian context, belief refers to accepting the truth of who God is, what He has done through Jesus Christ, and what He continues to do in the world. The Bible is filled with examples where belief is the first response to God's revelation.

John 3:16 is perhaps the most famous verse emphasizing the importance of belief:

"For God so loved the world that He gave His one and only Son, that whoever believes in Him shall not perish but have eternal life."

In this verse, belief is the gateway to salvation. To believe in Jesus is to accept His identity as the Son of God and to trust in the saving power of His life, death, and resurrection. This belief opens the door to eternal life, but the verse does not imply that belief, in itself, completes the Christian experience.

Romans 10:9 similarly highlights the centrality of belief in salvation:

_"If you declare with your mouth, 'Jesus is Lord,' and believe in your heart that God raised him from the dead, you will be saved."

Here, belief in the resurrection of Jesus is tied to salvation. Believing that Jesus rose from the dead is an intellectual acceptance of the foundational truth of the gospel. Yet even in this passage, belief is paired with confession—a declaration of faith that flows from belief and reflects a personal commitment to Jesus.

The Limitation of Belief Alone

While belief is essential, the Bible also presents warnings about the limitations of belief without a corresponding trust or faith. James 2:19 gives a stark reminder of this:

"You believe that there is one God. Good! Even the demons believe that—and shudder."

This verse makes it clear that belief in God's existence, by itself, is not enough. Even demons, who oppose God, believe in His existence and power. Their belief does not lead to transformation or salvation because it is not accompanied by trust, submission, or faith. The demons acknowledge the truth of who God is, but their belief does not change their relationship with Him.

This passage forces us to confront the reality that mere intellectual acknowledgment of God's truth is insufficient for a genuine relationship with Him. Belief, when isolated from trust, love, and obedience, can be shallow and ineffective. As theologian A.W. Tozer once said, "A man can die of thirst while holding a cup of water if he does not drink it." Belief must be put into action through faith for it to transform a person's life.

Belief as the Foundation of Faith

Although belief alone is insufficient, it remains the foundation of faith. Faith builds upon belief, transforming it into something far more profound and life-changing. The New Testament consistently teaches that belief is the starting point, but it must grow into faith to produce spiritual fruit.

Hebrews 11:6 emphasizes the connection between belief and faith:

"And without faith, it is impossible to please God, because anyone who comes to Him must believe that He exists and that He rewards those who earnestly seek Him."

This verse presents belief as the prerequisite to faith—it must begin with the acknowledgment that God exists. But the verse also pushes us further by stating that faith involves more than just believing in God's existence; it includes seeking Him, trusting that He rewards those who diligently pursue Him. Faith transforms belief from a static acknowledgment into a dynamic relationship with God.

Consider the example of the disciple Thomas, known for doubting the resurrection of Jesus until he could see and touch the wounds in Jesus' hands. In John 20:25, Thomas famously said:

"Unless I see the nail marks in His hands and put my finger where the nails were, and put my hand into His side, I will not believe."

When Jesus appeared to Thomas and offered him the evidence he needed, Thomas responded with belief, saying, _"My Lord and my God!"_ (John 20:28). Jesus then told Thomas, _"Because you have seen me, you have believed; blessed are those who have not seen and yet have believed"_ (John 20:29)._ Jesus' statement highlights the progression from belief based on physical evidence to a deeper, more blessed faith that trusts in God without needing to see.

Belief Leading to Faith

Belief is not meant to be the stopping point of the Christian journey. Once a person believes in the truth of God, that belief should naturally lead to faith. Faith, as discussed in the previous chapter, involves trust, commitment, and reliance on God. It is a response that goes beyond the intellect and engages the heart and will.

Mark 9:24 provides a poignant example of belief growing into faith. A father, desperate for Jesus to heal his son, says,

"I do believe; help me overcome my unbelief!"

This father's cry reveals the tension that many Christians experience. He believes in Jesus' power to heal, but he recognizes that his belief is incomplete—it needs to grow into faith. His request for help demonstrates that belief alone is not sufficient; he seeks a deeper trust in Jesus that goes beyond intellectual acknowledgment.

Faith transforms belief into action. In Matthew 14:28-31, Peter demonstrates how belief and faith work together. When Jesus walked on water, Peter believed that Jesus could enable him to do the same. He stepped out of the boat in faith, acting on his belief in Jesus' power. But when he saw the wind and waves, he became afraid and began to sink. Jesus rescued Peter and said, _"You of little faith, why did you doubt?"

Peter's belief in Jesus was real, but his faith wavered when fear overcame him. This story illustrates that belief is the starting point, but faith requires a deeper trust that holds firm even in the face of doubt and adversity.

Why Belief Must Be Paired with Faith

The Bible teaches that belief must be paired with faith for a transformative relationship with God. Belief alone acknowledges the truth of who God is, but faith commits to that truth in a way that shapes how we live. Faith turns belief into a lived experience, one that trusts in God's promises, follows His commands, and perseveres through trials.

In John 14:1, Jesus tells His disciples:

"Do not let your hearts be troubled. You believe in God; believe also in me."

Here, Jesus draws a distinction between believing in God and trusting in Him personally. The disciples' belief in God's existence was not enough to calm their fears; they needed to trust in Jesus' love, power, and authority over their circumstances. This distinction between belief and faith is essential for the Christian life. Belief acknowledges God's existence and power, but faith entrusts one's life to God, even in times of uncertainty or suffering.

James 2:17 emphasizes the necessity of faith-driven action:

"In the same way, faith by itself, if it is not accompanied by action, is dead."

Faith that flows from belief compels action. Belief acknowledges the truth of the gospel, but faith lives out that truth in practical ways. Faith manifests in obedience, service, love, and trust in God's will. Without faith, belief remains static and lifeless, unable to produce the transformative effect that God desires.

Believing is the starting point of the Christian journey, and it is essential for salvation. It represents the intellectual acceptance of God's truth, the gospel, and the reality of Jesus Christ. However, belief on its own is not enough for a dynamic, transformative relationship with God. Belief must lead to faith, a deeper trust that involves commitment, obedience, and reliance on God's promises.

As we have seen, belief alone can be as shallow as the acknowledgment that even demons have of God's existence. True Christian belief, however, is meant to grow into faith that sustains and empowers the believer. Faith takes belief and turns it into a lived reality, one that transforms both the individual and their relationship with God.

Believing is where the journey begins, but faith is where it flourishes. Faith breathes life into belief, turning it into a foundation upon which the whole Christian life is built. As we continue in this study, we will explore how this faith grows and manifests in the life of a believer, and why it is crucial for a thriving relationship with God.

Expository Bible Study and Commentary with Strong's Concordance": "believing" as the foundation of faith in the Christian journey"

In this chapter, we explore the concept of "believing" as the foundation of faith in the Christian journey. Belief is where many begin their spiritual walk, accepting the truths of the gospel intellectually and recognizing God's reality. However, while belief initiates one's journey, faith expands beyond belief, encompassing trust, transformation, and commitment. Through a deeper analysis, using Strong's Concordance, we examine belief as the entry point to faith and understand its essential role within the Bible.

Key Terms in Strong's Concordance:

1. Believe (πιστεύω, pisteuo) - Strong's G4100

2. Faith (πίστις, pistis) - Strong's G4102

3. Confession (ὁμολογέω, homologeo) - Strong's G3670

4. Acknowledge (ἐπίγνωσις, epignosis) - Strong's G1922

5. Obedience (ὑπακοή, hypakoe) - Strong's G5218

Expository Bible Study and Commentary

John 3:16 - Belief as the Starting Point for Salvation

"For God so loved the world, that He gave His only begotten Son, that whosoever believes (pisteuo - G4100) in Him should not perish, but have everlasting life."

- Strong's Analysis: "Pisteuo" (G4100) refers to trust, acceptance, or acknowledgment of a truth.

- Commentary: John 3:16 is one of the most quoted verses in the New Testament, highlighting belief as the necessary response to God's love. Here, "pisteuo" involves more than mere intellectual agreement; it points to a deep, accepting trust in Jesus as the source of eternal life. This initial belief forms the basis upon which salvation is received, but it is still only the entry point into a fuller life of faith. Belief alone, while essential, does not capture the entirety of faith that God desires.

Romans 10:9 - Confession and Belief as the Foundation of Salvation

"If you confess (homologeo - G3670) with your mouth the Lord Jesus and believe (pisteuo - G4100) in your heart that God has raised Him from the dead, you will be saved."

- Strong's Analysis: "Homologeo" (G3670) means to declare openly or acknowledge, while "pisteuo" (G4100) refers to a belief that involves conviction.

- Commentary: Romans 10:9 suggests that belief must extend beyond private thought into public acknowledgment. True belief entails an inner conviction of Jesus' Lordship and resurrection, accompanied by an outward confession. This verse emphasizes the integration of belief with an active, external demonstration of faith. Theologically, it shows that belief begins within but naturally seeks outward expression, solidifying belief as an initial commitment that invites further spiritual depth and growth.

James 2:19 - Intellectual Belief Alone is Insufficient

"You believe (pisteuo - G4100) that there is one God. You do well. Even the demons believe—and tremble!"

- Strong's Analysis: Here, "pisteuo" indicates an acknowledgment of truth, without the element of trust or commitment.

- Commentary: James uses a striking example to clarify that mere intellectual belief is not sufficient for salvation or relationship with God. Demons "believe" in God's existence, yet their belief lacks the personal trust and commitment that defines true faith. This highlights that belief, while foundational, is not the same as saving faith, as it lacks the relational and transformative elements required for salvation. James cautions readers that belief alone, without commitment and change, falls short of true discipleship.

Acts 16:31 - Believing in Jesus for Salvation

"So they said, 'Believe (pisteuo - G4100) on the Lord Jesus Christ, and you will be saved, you and your household.'"

- Strong's Analysis: "Pisteuo" here involves a form of trust that leads to salvation, not simply an acknowledgment of Jesus' existence.

- Commentary: The response of Paul and Silas to the Philippian jailer points to belief as a saving action. Here, "pisteuo" is an invitation to place trust in Jesus as Savior. This trust implies reliance on Jesus for salvation and surrender to His authority. It is the entry point through which one begins a relationship with Christ, marking the transition from intellectual acknowledgment to a transformative belief that draws the believer into God's grace.

Hebrews 11:6 - Belief as Essential to Pleasing God

"But without faith (pistis - G4102) it is impossible to please Him, for he who comes to God must believe (pisteuo - G4100) that He is, and that He is a rewarder of those who diligently seek Him."

- Strong's Analysis: "Pisteuo" denotes the recognition of God's existence, while "pistis" (G4102) encompasses a trusting and active faith.

- Commentary: This verse emphasizes that faith, built on the foundation of belief, is essential to a relationship with God. Believing that "God is" forms the beginning of faith, as it establishes the understanding of God's existence and goodness. However, true faith moves beyond belief, encompassing an active pursuit of God's will. This passage underscores the progression from believing in God's existence to actively seeking Him and aligning with His promises—a key theological distinction between simple belief and the fullness of faith.

Mark 9:23-24 - Belief Requires Growth in Faith

"Jesus said to him, 'If you can believe (pisteuo - G4100), all things are possible to him who believes.' Immediately the father of the child cried out and said with tears, 'Lord, I believe; help my unbelief!'"

- Strong's Analysis: "Pisteuo" here indicates a fledgling belief that recognizes its own limitations.

- Commentary: The father's response to Jesus reflects a belief that is genuine yet incomplete, seeking growth. This verse illustrates how belief often begins as an initial acknowledgment that requires further nurturing and strengthening. Theologically, it shows that belief is a starting point, which the believer must consciously develop into a fuller faith. In this case, the man's honesty about his partial belief invites Jesus' compassion and help, demonstrating that God welcomes those who seek to deepen their belief into enduring faith.

Theological Reflections on Belief

1. Belief as Intellectual Acknowledgment: Belief, or "pisteuo," is the acknowledgment of truth. As seen in Romans 10:9, it starts in the heart and can lead to salvation, but it is also an intellectual response to God's revelation. Belief

recognizes God's truth, forming the foundation on which faith can be built.

2. The Limitations of Belief Alone: Passages like James 2:19 show that belief alone, while necessary, is insufficient for a true relationship with God. Belief must progress into faith, as belief alone does not inherently contain trust, commitment, or obedience.

3. Belief as a Stepping-Stone to Faith: In Hebrews 11:6, belief forms the starting point for faith, as it affirms God's existence and His reward for seekers. It is a necessary precursor to faith that moves into a deeper trust and commitment.

4. Faith and Belief in Salvation: In verses like Acts 16:31, belief initiates the path to salvation, as it invites one to place trust in Jesus as Lord and Savior. Belief is the necessary step into a relational faith, where belief transforms into trust, and faith becomes the guiding force in a believer's life.

5. Belief as Growth Potential: In Mark 9:24, the father's statement "I believe, help my unbelief" illustrates that belief often begins with an openness to God but recognizes its need for growth. Belief, thus, is the starting point that encourages the believer to move into a fuller, more active faith.

Belief is essential in the Christian life, marking the initial acknowledgment of God's truth and the beginning of one's journey toward salvation. However, as shown throughout these scriptures, belief alone is not sufficient to sustain a relationship with God. Belief must grow and mature into faith—a faith that involves trust, action, and obedience. By examining belief through Strong's Concordance and biblical examples, we see belief as a dynamic beginning that, when nurtured, blossoms into a life-transforming faith.

CHAPTER 04

FAITH AS TRUST AND COMMITMENT

Faith, in its fullest expression, goes beyond merely believing in the truth of God's existence or His promises—it involves a profound trust in God's character and a commitment to align one's life with His will. This kind of faith transcends intellectual acknowledgment and demands a relationship of deep reliance on God, even when circumstances seem to challenge His promises. Biblical faith is built on trust and sustained by a commitment to follow God, no matter the cost.

In this chapter, we will explore how faith is inseparable from trust and commitment, drawing from the examples of Abraham and other biblical figures who exemplified faith in action. Their stories reveal that faith is not simply about believing that God can act, but trusting that He will act in His time and committing our lives to His purposes regardless of immediate outcomes.

Faith as Trust: The Foundation of Relationship

Trust is at the very core of biblical faith. Trust implies a personal relationship where one relies on the other to act faithfully and truthfully. In the Christian life, faith is grounded in the trustworthiness of God's character—His goodness, faithfulness, and ability to fulfill what He has promised. This trust is not blind but based on God's proven track record throughout history and His revelation in Scripture.

One of the clearest examples of faith as trust is found in the life of Abraham. Romans 4:3 tells us,

"Abraham believed God, and it was credited to him as righteousness."

Abraham's belief in God was not simply an intellectual agreement with a set of propositions; it was trust that God would fulfill His promise to make Abraham the father of many nations, even though Abraham and his wife Sarah were well beyond childbearing years. This trust is what God counted as righteousness—it was not Abraham's actions but his trust in God's ability to keep His word that made him righteous before God.

Abraham's trust in God was demonstrated in his willingness to leave his homeland and journey to an unknown land based on God's promise. Hebrews 11:8 recounts this:

"By faith Abraham obeyed when he was called to go out to the place which he would receive as an inheritance. And he went out, not knowing where he was going."

This is the essence of trust. Abraham did not have all the details of where he was going or how things would unfold, but he trusted God enough to obey and take action. Faith, therefore, is more than belief; it involves trusting God in the face of uncertainty and walking forward in obedience, confident in God's direction.

Faith as Commitment: Aligning with God's Will

Faith also requires commitment—an ongoing decision to align one's life with the will of God. This commitment is not always easy, especially when circumstances make it difficult to see how God's promises will be fulfilled. Yet true faith persists, trusting that God's timing and wisdom surpass our own understanding.

The story of Abraham's near-sacrifice of Isaac illustrates faith as commitment. In Genesis 22:2, God instructed Abraham to sacrifice his son Isaac, through whom God had promised to establish a great nation. Despite the apparent contradiction between God's promise and His command, Abraham demonstrated a steadfast commitment to God's will, trusting that God would provide a way to fulfill His promise.

Hebrews 11:17-19 reflects on Abraham's faith in this moment:

"By faith Abraham, when God tested him, offered Isaac as a sacrifice. He who had embraced the promises was about to sacrifice his one and only son, even though God had said to him, 'It is through Isaac that your offspring will be reckoned.' Abraham reasoned that God could even raise the dead, and so in a manner of speaking, he did receive Isaac back from death."

Here we see the depth of Abraham's commitment to God. He trusted so completely in God's ability to keep His promises that he was willing to offer up Isaac, believing that God could even raise him from the dead if necessary. Abraham's faith was not passive; it involved a costly commitment to God's will, even when it was difficult to understand.

Faith, therefore, is not a one-time decision but an ongoing commitment to follow God's lead, trusting that His plan is better than our own. This is reflected in Jesus' call to His disciples to take up their cross daily and follow Him (Luke 9:23). Faith involves surrendering our will to God's, even when it requires sacrifice or goes against our natural inclinations.

Trust in God's Promises Amid Uncertainty

Faith as trust becomes particularly vital in times of uncertainty, when the fulfillment of God's promises seems distant or even impossible. The Bible is filled with examples of people who trusted in God's promises despite the circumstances, demonstrating that true faith holds firm even when the outcome is not immediately visible.

One of the most powerful examples of this is the story of Shadrach, Meshach, and Abednego, who refused to bow to King Nebuchadnezzar's golden image, even though it meant being thrown into a fiery furnace. Their faith was not based on a guaranteed outcome, but on their trust in God's ability to deliver them. They said to the king,

"If we are thrown into the blazing furnace, the God we serve is able to deliver us from it, and He will deliver us from Your Majesty's hand. But even if He does not, we want you to know, Your Majesty, that we will not serve your gods or worship the image of gold you have set up." (Daniel 3:17-18)

This passage highlights an important aspect of faith: it trusts in God's character and His power, but it does not demand a specific outcome. Shadrach, Meshach, and Abednego trusted that God could save them, but their commitment to God was not contingent on whether He would intervene in the way they hoped. True faith maintains trust in God's goodness and wisdom, even when circumstances are difficult or confusing.

This kind of faith was also exemplified by Job, who famously said,

"Though He slay me, yet will I trust Him." (Job 13:15)

Job's faith did not depend on God's blessings or favorable circumstances. He trusted God's sovereignty and goodness, even in the midst of immense suffering. This trust is what sustained him and allowed him to remain faithful despite his trials.

Faith as Action: Living According to God's Will

Faith, when rooted in trust and commitment, naturally leads to action. James 2:17 reminds us that:

"Faith by itself, if it is not accompanied by action, is dead."

True faith compels us to live in alignment with God's will. It is not merely a belief system but a way of life. This is why faith and works are so closely connected in the Bible. Our actions flow out of our faith in God, demonstrating our trust in His promises and our commitment to His commands.

Consider the example of Rahab, whose faith led her to hide the Israelite spies in Jericho, even at great personal risk. James 2:25 says:

"In the same way, was not even Rahab the prostitute considered righteous for what she did when she gave lodging to the spies and sent them off in a different direction?"

Rahab's faith was not just intellectual; it moved her to take action, trusting in the God of Israel and aligning herself with His purposes. Faith, therefore, is not passive; it involves active obedience, even when it requires risk or sacrifice.

Faith and Patience: Trusting in God's Timing

A key component of faith is patience—waiting on God's timing. Often, the fulfillment of God's promises does not happen immediately, and faith requires us to trust Him in the waiting. Hebrews 6:12 encourages believers to imitate those who,

"through faith and patience, inherit the promises."

Abraham had to wait decades before God's promise of a son was fulfilled, and even after Isaac's birth, the full scope of God's promise—to make Abraham the father of many nations—would take generations to unfold. During this waiting period, Abraham's faith was tested, but he remained committed to God's promise, trusting that God's timing was perfect.

Faith as trust and commitment, therefore, involves patience. It requires us to remain faithful, even when we do not immediately see the results of God's promises. This kind of faith rests in the assurance that God is working all things together for good (Romans 8:28), even when we cannot see how.

Faith as the Heart of Trust and Commitment

Faith is more than belief in the truth of God's promises; it is a deep trust in His character and a commitment to live according to His will, even when we do not understand or see the fulfillment of His promises. Trust is the essence of faith—it involves relying on God's faithfulness and His ability to do what He has promised. Commitment, meanwhile, is the action that faith inspires, compelling us to live in obedience to God's commands.

Throughout Scripture, faith is demonstrated not by people who simply believe in God's existence, but by those who trust in His promises and commit their lives to His purposes. From Abraham to Job, from Rahab to the disciples, faith has always involved trusting in God's character and His timing, even when circumstances seem difficult or unclear.

In the Christian life, faith calls us to trust in God's goodness and wisdom, to commit ourselves to His will, and to walk in obedience to His commands, no matter the challenges we face. This kind of faith pleases God and transforms us into people who live not by sight, but by trust in His unseen promises.

Expository Bible Study and Commentary with Strong's Concordance: "faith" as a deep trust and steadfast commitment to God

This chapter delves into "faith" as a deep trust and steadfast commitment to God. Faith, understood through biblical context, is far more than intellectual acceptance or momentary belief—it is a relational bond that expresses loyalty, reliance, and action. Figures like Abraham demonstrate faith as trust that guides decisions and life choices. Using Strong's Concordance, we analyze key words that show faith as an active and enduring trust, rooted in the commitment to God's promises and commands.

Key Terms in Strong's Concordance:

1. Faith (πίστις, pistis) - Strong's G4102

2. Trust (בטח, batach) - Strong's H982 (Old Testament Hebrew)

3. Commit (גָּלַל, galal) - Strong's H1556 (Old Testament Hebrew)

4. Faithful (πιστός, pistos) - Strong's G4103

5. Obedience (ὑπακοή, hypakoe) - Strong's G5218

Expository Bible Study and Commentary

Hebrews 11:1 - Faith as Substance and Evidence

"Now faith (pistis - G4102) is the substance of things hoped for, the evidence of things not seen."

- Strong's Analysis: "Pistis" (G4102) denotes faith as a firm conviction and assurance, indicating trust that gives reality to hope.

- Commentary: Hebrews 11:1 defines faith as something substantial—a confidence in God's promises. Faith here is both tangible ("substance") and persuasive ("evidence"), suggesting that faith itself acts as proof of God's unseen promises. This verse sets the foundation for understanding faith not only as belief but as active trust that brings assurance in God's faithfulness, despite the unseen. This concept of faith encourages believers to hold a deep-seated commitment to God, even when circumstances do not visibly confirm His promises.

Romans 4:3 - Abraham's Faith as Righteousness

"For what does the Scripture say? 'Abraham believed (pisteuo - G4100) God, and it was accounted to him for righteousness.'"

- Strong's Analysis: "Pisteuo" (G4100) involves a faith that implies reliance and fidelity, an allegiance to God's promises.

- Commentary: Abraham's faith exemplifies how trust becomes a defining feature of one's relationship with God. Abraham did not merely believe intellectually; his faith meant aligning his actions and decisions with his trust in God's covenant. His commitment was credited as righteousness, showing that trust in God carries divine approval and sets a model for faithful commitment. Abraham's journey reflects the depth of faith that moves beyond belief to shape one's entire life, suggesting that true faith leads to an abiding commitment to follow God, regardless of external validation.

Proverbs 3:5-6 - Trust in the Lord with All Your Heart

"Trust (batach - H982) in the Lord with all your heart, and lean not on your own understanding; in all your ways acknowledge Him, and He shall direct your paths."

- Strong's Analysis: "Batach" (H982) means to trust securely or rely upon, showing a deep confidence in God's guidance.

- Commentary: Proverbs 3:5-6 defines the nature of trust as a complete reliance on God rather than on personal reasoning. Faith here is shown as a commitment to God's direction, even when circumstances or personal understanding suggest otherwise. Trusting "with all your heart" emphasizes the wholehearted nature of faith, which surrenders personal control and allows God to lead. This passage conveys that faith involves trusting God's character and promises, developing a relationship of continual guidance and reliance.

James 2:17-18 - Faith Proved Through Works

"Thus also faith (pistis - G4102) by itself, if it does not have works, is dead. But someone will say, 'You have faith, and I have works.' Show me your faith without your works, and I will show you my faith by my works."

- Strong's Analysis: "Pistis" indicates active faith, one that must be substantiated by action.

- Commentary: James emphasizes that faith, if genuine, will result in visible action. Faith without works lacks the essence of trust and commitment, as true faith compels believers to act upon their beliefs. Works become the expression of trust, showcasing the authenticity of one's commitment to God. This passage illustrates that faith as trust requires commitment to God's instructions, and without works, faith is incomplete. Faith is not static; it is demonstrated and fortified through obedience and visible actions.

Psalm 37:5 - Committing Your Way to the Lord

"Commit (galal - H1556) your way to the Lord; trust (batach - H982) also in Him, and He shall bring it to pass."

- Strong's Analysis: "Galal" (H1556) means to roll onto, implying surrender and dedication, while "batach" reflects secure trust.

- Commentary: Psalm 37:5 suggests that commitment to God involves both surrender and trust. The Hebrew term "galal" conveys rolling one's concerns onto God, signifying a complete relinquishment of personal control. This type of faith entails entrusting God with one's life path, resting in the assurance that God will fulfill His promises. The verse portrays commitment as more than passive hope; it is an active and intentional decision to place one's future in God's hands. Faith, as trust and commitment, aligns one's life direction with God's purposes, creating a partnership of dependence and security.

Theological Reflections on Faith as Trust and Commitment

1. Faith as Active Trust: Faith in Scripture is often defined through actions and reliance on God's promises. Hebrews 11:1 presents faith as an assurance that grounds one's hope, reinforcing that trust is integral to faith. Trust as part of faith compels believers to live confidently in God's provision, knowing that God's promises are reliable.

2. Faith as Covenant Commitment: Faith is not simply belief but includes a relational component, as demonstrated by Abraham's faith in Romans 4:3. His trust in God's covenantal promises was not a one-time event but a lifetime

commitment. This deep commitment illustrates that faith is relational, involving a willingness to trust God's guidance for one's entire life.

3. Faith Manifested Through Obedience: Faith that trusts in God naturally leads to actions that align with God's will. James 2:17-18 shows that faith without corresponding actions is incomplete. Works become the evidence of trust, and true faith is demonstrated through a life committed to following God's instructions.

4. Commitment as Surrender and Dependency: Psalm 37:5 illustrates faith as a relationship of trust and surrender. Faith here is shown as "rolling" our lives onto God, entrusting our ways to Him. This act of surrender is a vital part of faith, indicating that trust requires not only confidence but also relinquishment of personal control.

5. Faith in Relationship with God: Faith as trust and commitment transforms belief into a dynamic relationship with God. Trust involves both acknowledging God's sovereignty and actively participating in His purposes. Commitment to God implies a lifelong devotion, creating a foundation for a relationship that endures beyond belief.

Practical Application of Faith as Trust and Commitment

- Faith in Action: Cultivate a faith that moves beyond belief by actively engaging in works that reflect trust in God.

Whether through acts of service, generosity, or discipleship, let your actions mirror your commitment to God.

- Daily Surrender: Each day, practice surrendering areas of your life to God. Reflect on the areas where you need to "roll your burdens" onto Him and invite His guidance over your plans.

- Meditation on God's Promises: Spend time each day meditating on specific promises in Scripture. Allow these promises to strengthen your trust and commitment, helping you develop a faith that is grounded in God's faithfulness.

- Community Accountability: Join with other believers who exemplify a life of trust and commitment to God. Fellowship and accountability will help strengthen your faith, encouraging you to remain committed to God's will.

Faith as trust and commitment moves beyond intellectual belief to become a powerful relational bond with God. True faith compels believers to surrender their lives, demonstrating trust through obedience and dependence. Through trust, commitment, and action, faith manifests as the essence of the Christian walk, guiding believers in a journey of reliance on God's promises and alignment with His will.

CHAPTER 05

THE RELATIONSHIP BETWEEN FAITH AND BELIEF

Faith and belief are often used interchangeably, but they hold distinct roles in the Christian life. Belief, in its essence, is the acceptance of truth—acknowledging certain facts or propositions as real. Faith, on the other hand, is much more comprehensive. It involves not only belief but also trust, reliance, and a commitment to act on that belief. While belief is foundational, faith transforms it into a living, dynamic relationship with God.

In this chapter, we will explore the relationship between faith and belief, highlighting how belief is essential but insufficient without faith. Through biblical examples, we will see how belief transitions into faith, and how faith grows beyond mere intellectual acknowledgment into trust, obedience, and action.

Belief as the Foundation of Faith

Belief is the starting point for faith. It is an intellectual acceptance of truth, whether that truth is the existence of God, the reality of Jesus Christ's death and resurrection, or the promises found in Scripture. Belief is necessary for salvation, as seen in John 3:16:

"For God so loved the world that He gave His one and only Son, that whoever believes in Him shall not perish but have eternal life."

In this well-known verse, belief in Jesus is presented as the path to eternal life. Belief is the initial step of the Christian journey, acknowledging the truth of who Jesus is and what He has done. However, belief alone does not encompass the fullness of faith. Even the demons believe in God, yet they do not have saving faith. As James 2:19 says:

"You believe that there is one God. Good! Even the demons believe that—and shudder."

James makes it clear that belief alone, even in the existence of God, is insufficient. The demons believe, but their belief does not lead to trust, reliance, or salvation. This verse illustrates that belief is necessary, but without faith—without trust and commitment—it remains incomplete.

Faith as the Fulfillment of Belief

Faith, as we have discussed in previous chapters, builds on belief but goes beyond it. Faith transforms belief into something living and active. It involves trusting in God's character, relying on His promises, and acting on His word. Faith is belief in action, where trust in God leads to obedience and a life committed to following Him.

A key example of the progression from belief to faith is found in the story of Thomas, one of Jesus' disciples. After Jesus' resurrection, Thomas struggled to believe the testimony of the other disciples, who had seen the risen Christ. In John 20:24-25, Thomas famously declared,

"Unless I see the nail marks in His hands and put my finger where the nails were, and put my hand into His side, I will not believe."

Thomas' statement reveals a common struggle—the desire for tangible evidence before fully believing. Though Thomas intellectually acknowledged the possibility of Jesus' resurrection, he lacked the faith to trust without seeing. When Jesus later appeared to Thomas, He invited him to touch the wounds in His hands and side. Upon seeing and touching Jesus, Thomas responded,

"My Lord and my God!" (John 20:28).

Here we see the transition from belief to faith. Thomas moved from a place of doubt to a place of trust and commitment. His belief in the resurrection became more than intellectual acknowledgment—it became personal faith in Jesus as Lord and God. Jesus then said to Thomas,

"Because you have seen me, you have believed; blessed are those who have not seen and yet have believed." (John 20:29).

This blessing highlights the nature of faith: it often requires trusting in what we cannot see. True faith is not dependent on physical evidence but rests on trust in God's character and His word. Thomas's journey illustrates how belief can lead to faith, but faith involves a deeper trust and commitment to God's promises, even when they are unseen.

How Belief Grows into Faith

Belief and faith are closely related, and belief often serves as the seed from which faith grows. However, belief alone cannot sustain a Christian life. Faith is what moves us from intellectual acknowledgment to a life of trust and reliance on God. The following aspects of faith demonstrate how belief matures into a deep, living trust in God:

1. Trust in God's Character:

True faith requires trusting in God's character, even when circumstances are difficult. In Proverbs 3:5-6, we are encouraged to:

"Trust in the Lord with all your heart and lean not on your own understanding; in all your ways submit to Him, and He will make your paths straight."

Belief acknowledges that God exists, but faith trusts that God is good, faithful, and just, even when we do not fully understand His ways. Faith invites us to lean not on our limited understanding but to trust that God's wisdom and plans are far greater than our own.

2. Relying on God's Promises:

Faith involves relying on God's promises, trusting that what He has spoken will come to pass, even if we cannot see it immediately. In Hebrews 11:1, we find one of the clearest definitions of faith:

"Now faith is confidence in what we hope for and assurance about what we do not see."

Faith grows from belief into reliance on the unseen promises of God. Abraham is a powerful example of this in the Bible. God promised Abraham that he would be the father of many nations, yet Abraham and his wife Sarah were old and had no children. Despite the apparent impossibility of the situation, Abraham trusted in God's promise. Romans 4:20-21 describes Abraham's faith:

"Yet he did not waver through unbelief regarding the promise of God, but was strengthened in his faith and gave glory to God, being fully persuaded that God had power to do what He had promised."

Abraham's belief in God's promise grew into faith as he relied on God's power and faithfulness. Even when circumstances made the fulfillment of the promise seem unlikely, Abraham trusted in God's ability to bring it to pass.

3. Action as an Expression of Faith:

Faith is not just an internal conviction; it is expressed through action. As James 2:17 says:

"In the same way, faith by itself, if it is not accompanied by action, is dead."

Faith manifests in obedience to God's commands. The story of Noah provides a clear example of this. Noah believed God's warning about the coming flood, but his faith was demonstrated through his obedience in building the ark. Hebrews 11:7 says:

"By faith Noah, when warned about things not yet seen, in holy fear built an ark to save his family. By his faith he condemned the world and became heir of the righteousness that is in keeping with faith."

Noah's belief in God's warning moved him to action. His faith was not passive but active, leading him to build the ark and prepare for the fulfillment of God's word. This demonstrates that faith goes beyond belief—it leads to trust that is lived out through obedience.

Belief Without Faith: The Warning of Incomplete Belief

While belief is necessary, the Bible warns that belief without faith is insufficient. In James 2:14, we are asked:

"What good is it, my brothers and sisters, if someone claims to have faith but has no deeds? Can such faith save them?"

James's question is rhetorical, pointing out that mere intellectual belief without faith—faith that results in action—is incomplete. Believing that God exists or even that Jesus is the Son of God is not enough if that belief does not lead to a transformed life. True faith compels us to act, to trust, and to follow God's will.

Jesus Himself warned against superficial belief in the parable of the sower. In Luke 8:13, Jesus speaks of those who hear the word of God and believe it for a time, but because they lack deep roots, they fall away when testing comes. This illustrates that belief, while essential, needs to grow into faith that can withstand trials and difficulties.

The Dynamic Relationship Between Faith and Belief

The relationship between faith and belief is dynamic. Belief is the starting point, the intellectual acknowledgment of

God's truth. But faith goes beyond belief—it trusts in God's character, relies on His promises, and leads to action. Without faith, belief remains incomplete, lacking the depth and power to transform lives.

As we have seen through the examples of Thomas, Abraham, Noah, and others, belief serves as the foundation for faith, but it must be nurtured into trust and obedience. Faith takes what we believe and compels us to live according to those beliefs, even in the face of uncertainty or difficulty.

In the Christian life, belief is where we begin, but faith is where we are called to grow. True faith turns belief into a relationship with God that is marked by trust, reliance, and action. This kind of faith pleases God and enables us to live fully in the promises of His word.

Expository Bible Study and Commentary with Strong's Concordance: Examining the relationship between faith and belief

In examining the relationship between faith and belief, we encounter two interconnected yet distinct concepts in the Bible. Belief, or accepting the truth of a statement or fact, is foundational to faith. However, faith goes beyond mere belief to include trust, commitment, and action based on that belief. Through the lens of Strong's Concordance, we can explore how the Bible differentiates between faith and belief, revealing how belief forms the basis of faith, which in turn leads to a transformative relationship with God.

Key Terms in Strong's Concordance

1. Faith (πίστις, pistis) - Strong's G4102

2. Believe (πιστεύω, pisteuo) - Strong's G4100

3. Obedience (ὑπακοή, hypakoe) - Strong's G5218

4. Unbelief (ἄπιστος, apistos) - Strong's G571

5. Righteousness (δικαιοσύνη, dikaiosyne) - Strong's G1343

Expository Bible Study and Commentary

John 20:29 - Blessed are Those Who Have Not Seen and Yet Have Believed

"Jesus said to him, 'Thomas, because you have seen Me, you have believed (pisteuo - G4100). Blessed are those who have not seen and yet have believed.'"

- Strong's Analysis: "Pisteuo" (G4100) signifies belief or trust, implying an acceptance of truth and confidence.

- Commentary: This verse contrasts the belief that comes from seeing with the faith that arises in the absence of physical evidence. Jesus acknowledges that while Thomas believed because he saw, true faith often requires trust without tangible proof. Belief here is shown as foundational to faith, but faith transcends belief when it persists without physical confirmation. Jesus pronounces a blessing on those who believe without seeing, emphasizing that faith grows stronger as it goes beyond initial belief.

James 2:19 - Even the Demons Believe and Tremble

"You believe (pisteuo - G4100) that there is one God. You do well. Even the demons believe—and tremble!"

- Strong's Analysis: "Pisteuo" here refers to an intellectual assent or acknowledgment of truth.

- Commentary: James stresses that belief alone, even in the existence of God, is insufficient for salvation or transformation. The demons "believe" yet remain opposed to God, illustrating that belief without faith lacks the relational trust and obedience required in a relationship with God. This passage underscores that faith involves a deeper commitment and response beyond simple acknowledgment; it requires a dedication to align one's actions and life with God's will.

Hebrews 11:6 - Without Faith, It Is Impossible to Please God

"But without faith (pistis - G4102) it is impossible to please Him, for he who comes to God must believe (pisteuo - G4100) that He is, and that He is a rewarder of those who diligently seek Him."

- Strong's Analysis: "Pistis" represents faith as a relational trust, while "pisteuo" refers to initial belief or acknowledgment.

- Commentary: This verse highlights the necessary progression from belief to faith. To please God, one must first believe in His existence and character. However, faith extends beyond belief to include trust in God's goodness and an ongoing commitment to seek Him. This verse explains why faith is essential to a relationship with God—faith implies an active pursuit and trust, demonstrating that belief alone does not capture the relational depth that faith entails.

Romans 10:9 - Belief in the Heart and Confession

"If you confess with your mouth the Lord Jesus and believe (pisteuo - G4100) in your heart that God has raised Him from the dead, you will be saved."

- Strong's Analysis: "Pisteuo" here indicates a heart-level belief, suggesting commitment beyond intellectual agreement.

- Commentary: This passage points to belief as essential for salvation but notes that this belief is meant to be profound, originating from the heart. Paul emphasizes that salvation arises not only from intellectual acceptance but from a deep-seated trust in Jesus' resurrection, which transforms and redeems the believer. This heart-based belief lays the foundation for faith, which will naturally lead to outward confession and alignment with God's will.

Mark 9:24 - Help My Unbelief!

"Immediately the father of the child cried out and said with tears, 'Lord, I believe (pisteuo - G4100); help my unbelief (apistos - G571)!'"

- Strong's Analysis: "Pisteuo" refers to trust or belief, while "apistos" indicates doubt or a lack of confidence.

- Commentary: The plea in Mark 9:24 captures the internal struggle between belief and doubt. The father's confession reflects an initial belief, yet he longs for the faith that overcomes uncertainty. This illustrates that faith matures as belief grows stronger and more confident in God's power. His request, "Help my unbelief," reflects the human condition—belief can coexist with doubt, but faith strengthens as it addresses these areas of unbelief through reliance on God. This verse suggests that faith is dynamic, growing as initial belief is nurtured into confident trust.

Theological Reflections on the Relationship Between Faith and Belief

1. Belief as the Foundation of Faith: Belief is often the starting point in the journey of faith. John 20:29 and Romans 10:9 show that belief establishes the basic acceptance of truth

and the recognition of God's existence and power. Yet, belief alone is incomplete. True faith transforms belief into trust, commitment, and an active relationship with God. Faith builds upon belief, developing a depth of reliance and assurance.

2. Faith as Relational and Action-Oriented: Where belief acknowledges truth, faith engages that truth relationally, leading to obedience and trust. Hebrews 11:6 reveals that faith is central to pleasing God, requiring trust that extends beyond mere belief. In this way, faith encourages ongoing commitment and involvement with God's promises. Faith, therefore, is relational and actionable, requiring dedication that surpasses intellectual understanding.

3. Faith Overcoming Doubt: Mark 9:24 exemplifies the reality that belief can coexist with doubt, but faith seeks to overcome unbelief through divine help. The father's plea to Jesus reflects a desire for stronger trust, demonstrating that faith is not static; it grows as belief deepens and doubts are addressed. This process shows that while belief initiates faith, faith matures by persevering through doubt.

4. Faith Evidenced Through Works: James 2:19 and Hebrews 11 emphasize that faith produces a response. Genuine faith is evidenced by actions that align with trust in God's will. Belief, while critical, is not a substitute for faith that leads to obedience. James highlights that even demons

believe, yet faith involves commitment, which is proven by how one lives in response to belief.

Practical Application of Faith and Belief in Christian Life

- Growing from Belief to Faith: To nurture faith, one must allow belief to extend into deeper commitment and trust in God's promises. This involves moving beyond intellectual acceptance to living in alignment with God's will.

- Addressing Doubts: Like the father in Mark 9:24, believers can bring their doubts to God, seeking His help to strengthen faith. This openness fosters growth from belief into resilient faith.

- Faith in Action: Practicing faith through obedience and works reveals a commitment that goes beyond belief. Acts of service, prayer, and adherence to God's guidance showcase faith as a lived experience.

This addendum emphasizes that belief and faith, while interconnected, are distinct. Belief accepts truth; faith acts upon it. This dynamic relationship between belief and faith deepens as initial belief evolves into a faithful, trust-filled commitment to God.

CHAPTER 06

BIBLICAL PERSPECTIVES ON FAITH AND BELIEVING

Throughout Scripture, faith and belief are intricately connected, yet distinct. While belief acknowledges the truth of who God is and what He has done, faith moves beyond this acknowledgment to trust, commitment, and action. In this chapter, we will examine key biblical passages that emphasize the relationship between faith and belief, demonstrating that true faith must be accompanied by works, trust, and reliance on God. We will also explore stories of individuals whose faith was demonstrated through their actions, showing how belief, when accompanied by faith, transforms lives.

James 2:14-26: Faith Without Works is Dead

One of the most explicit biblical discussions on the distinction between faith and belief comes from James 2:14-26, where James makes the case that faith must be accompanied by works to be considered genuine. He writes:

"What good is it, my brothers and sisters, if someone claims to have faith but has no deeds? Can such faith save them?" (James 2:14).

James confronts the idea that mere belief, or faith without action, is sufficient for salvation. He argues that faith is evidenced by works—practical, visible demonstrations of trust in God. Belief alone, while necessary, is incomplete if it does not lead to obedience and action.

James uses the example of Abraham to illustrate this point:

"Was not our father Abraham considered righteous for what he did when he offered his son Isaac on the altar? You see that his faith and his actions were working together, and his faith was made complete by what he did." (James 2:21-22).

Abraham believed in God's promises, but it was his willingness to act on that belief—by offering Isaac—that demonstrated the depth of his faith. Abraham's works, borne out of his faith, confirmed that his belief in God's promises was real and alive.

James goes even further by contrasting true faith with the shallow belief held by demons:

"You believe that there is one God. Good! Even the demons believe that—and shudder." (James 2:19).

Here, James underscores the insufficiency of belief without faith. Demons believe in God, acknowledging His existence and power, yet their belief does not lead to submission, trust, or obedience. This reinforces that true faith must lead to action—it must transform belief into works of obedience, reflecting a deep commitment to God's will.

The Centurion's Faith in Action: Matthew 8:5-13

One of the most powerful examples of belief being transformed into faith through action is the story of the Roman centurion in Matthew 8:5-13. The centurion approached Jesus, asking Him to heal his paralyzed servant, saying:

"Lord, my servant lies at home paralyzed, suffering terribly." (Matthew 8:6).

Jesus offered to come to the centurion's home to heal the servant, but the centurion, recognizing Jesus' authority, responded:

"Lord, I do not deserve to have you come under my roof. But just say the word, and my servant will be healed." (Matthew 8:8).

This statement reveals the depth of the centurion's faith. He not only believed that Jesus had the power to heal, but he trusted in Jesus' authority to the point that he did not require Jesus' physical presence. The centurion's belief was accompanied by a remarkable faith in Jesus' word, which led to Jesus' high praise:

"Truly I tell you, I have not found anyone in Israel with such great faith." (Matthew 8:10).

This story highlights how belief in Jesus' power grew into faith that trusted fully in His word and authority. The centurion's faith was not passive; it involved a deep conviction and trust that moved him to act on behalf of his servant. Jesus commended this faith because it was complete—belief paired with trust and action.

The Woman with the Issue of Blood: Mark 5:25-34

Another powerful biblical example of faith in action is the story of the woman with the issue of blood, found in Mark 5:25-34. This woman had suffered for twelve years from a bleeding disorder and had sought help from many doctors, but her condition had only worsened. When she heard about Jesus, she believed that He had the power to heal her. But her belief did not remain passive.

In an act of faith, she pushed through the crowd, thinking:

"If I just touch His clothes, I will be healed." (Mark 5:28).

Her belief in Jesus' healing power led her to take bold action. She reached out and touched His cloak, and immediately, her bleeding stopped. Jesus, aware that power had gone out from Him, turned around and asked who had touched Him. The woman, trembling with fear, came forward and confessed what she had done.

Jesus responded with words that affirmed her faith:

"Daughter, your faith has healed you. Go in peace and be freed from your suffering." (Mark 5:34).

This story illustrates the dynamic relationship between belief and faith. The woman believed in Jesus' ability to heal, but her faith was demonstrated by her action—pressing through the crowd to touch His garment. Her faith led to healing, showing that belief alone is not enough; faith must be active, leading to a reliance on Jesus and a willingness to take steps based on that trust.

The Relationship Between Faith and Works: Further Biblical Examples

The Bible is filled with examples of how belief and faith are intertwined, with true faith always resulting in action. Consider the story of Rahab in Joshua 2. Rahab believed that the God of Israel was the true God and that He would give the Israelites victory over Jericho. But her belief alone was not enough to save her. Rahab acted on her belief by hiding the Israelite spies and helping them escape, risking her life in the process.

Her actions were a demonstration of her faith, as Hebrews 11:31 tells us:

"By faith the prostitute Rahab, because she welcomed the spies, was not killed with those who were disobedient."

Rahab's faith was made evident through her works—her belief in God led her to take courageous action, resulting in her salvation.

Another example is found in the story of Peter walking on water in Matthew 14:28-31. Peter believed that Jesus had the power to enable him to walk on water, but it was not until Peter stepped out of the boat that his faith was revealed. However, when Peter took his eyes off Jesus and focused on the wind and waves, he began to doubt and sink. This story shows how belief can falter without sustained faith, and how faith must be nurtured through continual trust in Jesus.

The Faith of Abraham: A Model of Belief and Action

Abraham is often held up as a model of faith in the Bible because his belief in God was consistently paired with action. God promised Abraham that he would be the father of many nations, but for years, that promise seemed impossible to fulfill because Abraham and Sarah had no children. Despite this, Abraham believed God's promise and acted in faith.

In Genesis 22, when God tested Abraham by commanding him to sacrifice Isaac, the son through whom God's promise was to be fulfilled, Abraham's faith was demonstrated by his willingness to obey. His belief in God's promises led to trust in God's ability to provide, even in the most challenging circumstances.

Hebrews 11:17-19 reflects on this moment of faith:

"By faith Abraham, when God tested him, offered Isaac as a sacrifice. He who had embraced the promises was about to sacrifice his one and only son, even though God had said to him, 'It is through Isaac that your offspring will be reckoned.' Abraham reasoned that God could even raise the dead, and so in a manner of speaking, he did receive Isaac back from death."

Abraham's faith was not a passive belief in God's promises but an active, trusting obedience, even when he could not see how God's plan would unfold. His faith transformed his belief into action, making him an exemplar of faith for generations to come.

The Interdependence of Faith and Belief

The biblical perspective on faith and belief reveals that belief is the foundation upon which faith is built, but true faith must go beyond belief to include trust, action, and commitment. Belief acknowledges the truth of God's existence, promises, and power, but faith takes this belief and translates it into trust and obedience.

From the centurion to the woman with the issue of blood, from Rahab to Abraham, the Bible shows that faith is always accompanied by action. It is not enough to merely believe; true faith compels us to live in alignment with God's will, trusting Him fully and acting on His promises.

As we reflect on these biblical examples, we are reminded that faith is the living response to belief. It is the outworking of our trust in God, demonstrated through our actions and obedience. Faith and belief are inseparable, but it is faith that transforms belief into a vibrant, dynamic relationship with God.

Supplements to Chapter 6: "Biblical Perspectives on Faith and Believing"

Expository Bible Study and Commentary with Strong's Concordance

In exploring the biblical perspectives on faith and belief, we delve into the multifaceted nature of these concepts in the context of scriptural teachings. The Bible illustrates that while belief acknowledges God's truth, faith engages that belief through commitment, trust, and action. Biblical accounts exemplify how faith and belief function in distinct ways, underscoring how belief initiates and faith activates a deep, relational bond with God.

Key Terms in Strong's Concordance

1. Faith (πίστις, pistis) - Strong's G4102

2. Believe (πιστεύω, pisteuo) - Strong's G4100

3. Unbelief (ἀπιστία, apistia) - Strong's G570

4. Trust (πεποίθησις, pepoithesis) - Strong's G4006

5. Works (ἔργον, ergon) - Strong's G2041

Expository Bible Study and Commentary

James 2:14-26 - Faith Without Works is Dead

"What does it profit, my brethren, if someone says he has faith but does not have works? Can faith save him? ... For as the body without the spirit is dead, so faith without works is dead also."

- Strong's Analysis: The word "faith" (pistis - G4102) here is used to denote trust that naturally results in action, while "works" (ergon - G2041) represents tangible actions reflecting one's faith.

- Commentary: James contrasts mere intellectual assent with genuine faith that is evidenced through actions. This passage clarifies that belief alone is insufficient for salvation. Faith is transformative, leading to obedience and good works. James emphasizes that faith is not passive; it compels the believer to act in alignment with God's will. This perspective establishes that belief initiates understanding, but faith, proven through works, confirms true commitment.

Hebrews 11:1 - Faith as Substance and Evidence

"Now faith (pistis - G4102) is the substance of things hoped for, the evidence of things not seen."

- Strong's Analysis: "Faith" (pistis - G4102) here implies assurance and conviction, conveying both a present reality ("substance") and future expectation ("evidence").

- Commentary: The writer of Hebrews presents faith as a present assurance in what is hoped for, a conviction in what is unseen. This definition of faith transcends belief in visible facts, illustrating that faith is a confident reliance on God's promises. Faith provides the believer with a tangible sense of certainty even in the absence of physical proof, portraying faith as a bridge between belief and experience.

Mark 9:23-24 - Faith and the Struggle with Unbelief

"Jesus said to him, 'If you can believe (pisteuo - G4100), all things are possible to him who believes.'

Immediately the father of the child cried out and said with tears, 'Lord, I believe; help my unbelief (apistia - G570)!'"

- Strong's Analysis: "Believe" (pisteuo - G4100) reflects initial trust or confidence, while "unbelief" (apistia - G570) suggests doubt or lack of faith.

- Commentary: This passage reveals the complexity of belief and faith, showing how they coexist with doubt. The father's plea highlights that faith may begin with belief, yet mature faith seeks God's help in areas of doubt. This account underscores that God responds to sincere belief even when accompanied by imperfect faith. This perspective provides a compassionate view of faith, where belief serves as a foundation that faith builds upon, overcoming doubt through divine assistance.

Matthew 8:5-13 - The Centurion's Faith

"When Jesus heard it, He marveled, and said to those who followed, 'Assuredly, I say to you, I have not found such great faith (pistis - G4102), not even in Israel!'"

- Strong's Analysis: "Faith" (pistis - G4102) here implies deep trust and confidence in Jesus' authority and power.

- Commentary: The centurion's story illustrates a profound example of faith that transcends simple belief. His confidence in Jesus' power to heal from afar demonstrates a deep trust without requiring physical evidence. This account demonstrates how true faith acknowledges God's authority and acts upon it, even when circumstances seem insurmountable. The centurion's faith reflects the maturity of belief, evolving into trust that fully rests on God's ability to act.

Luke 17:5-6 - Faith Like a Mustard Seed

"And the apostles said to the Lord, 'Increase our faith (pistis - G4102).' So the Lord said, 'If you have faith as a mustard seed, you can say to this mulberry tree, "Be pulled up by the roots and be planted in the sea," and it would obey you.'"

- Strong's Analysis: "Faith" (pistis - G4102) represents potential, emphasizing quality over quantity.

- Commentary: Jesus' response to the disciples teaches that even a small measure of genuine faith can yield great results. Faith, like a mustard seed, grows over time and transforms situations. Jesus emphasizes that the essence of faith lies not in its magnitude but in its authenticity and trust in God's power. This passage illustrates that faith, rooted in true belief, can overcome obstacles as it grows and matures.

Theological Reflections on Biblical Perspectives of Faith and Belief

1. Belief as Intellectual Assent and Foundation of Faith: Belief is the initial acknowledgment of God's truth, acting as the foundation upon which faith builds. In James 2, we see that belief is essential, yet insufficient by itself. True faith builds upon belief, moving toward a commitment that drives action. This foundational belief is necessary, but faith grows as it becomes relational and transformative.

2. Faith as Active Trust and Commitment: In passages like Hebrews 11:1, faith is defined as a present conviction and an active trust in God's promises. Faith goes beyond belief, compelling believers to live in anticipation of what is unseen. Biblical faith manifests through commitment and action, requiring a relational trust that rests in God's character. Where belief provides mental acceptance, faith initiates life change through deep-seated trust.

3. Faith and Unbelief Coexisting: The account of Mark 9 shows that belief can coexist with doubt, and faith seeks divine help to strengthen it. The father's plea, "Help my unbelief," reveals the tension believers often feel between what they know intellectually and what they struggle to trust fully. Faith addresses these areas of doubt, growing stronger through dependence on God's grace.

4. Faith Evidenced by Works: James 2 asserts that faith is incomplete without actions to confirm it. True faith aligns with God's will, producing works as evidence of its

authenticity. Biblical faith requires tangible actions that reflect inner conviction, demonstrating that genuine faith cannot remain hidden or inactive.

5. Faith Beyond Quantity—The Mustard Seed: In Luke 17, Jesus teaches that faith's potency is not in its size but in its genuine trust in God's power. Faith, even as small as a mustard seed, can lead to miraculous results. This perspective reveals that faith's effectiveness lies in its depth, rather than its magnitude, encouraging believers to cultivate an authentic and steadfast trust.

Practical Applications of Biblical Faith and Belief

- Growing Faith through Prayer and Scripture: The example of the father in Mark 9 illustrates that seeking God's help strengthens faith, particularly in areas of doubt. Regular prayer and immersion in Scripture deepen one's belief, nurturing a resilient faith.

- Faith in Action: Following James 2, believers are called to demonstrate their faith through actions that align with God's purposes. This calls for a proactive approach to faith, where belief is visible in how we live, serve, and respond to God's call.

- Overcoming Doubt: By acknowledging areas of unbelief and relying on God's strength, believers can transform initial belief into steadfast faith. Openness in addressing doubts promotes growth, fostering a mature faith that fully trusts in God's promises.

- Trusting in God's Character: The centurion's faith in Matthew 8 exemplifies trust in Jesus' authority and power. Believers are encouraged to develop a faith that rests not on circumstances but on God's unchanging character, transforming belief into a secure, active faith.

Biblical perspectives on faith and belief highlight the progression from intellectual acknowledgment to relational trust. Belief, while essential, is merely the foundation of faith, which grows through commitment, action, and trust. The Bible demonstrates that faith, when nurtured, transforms lives, allowing believers to live confidently in God's promises and actively in His service.

CHAPTER 07

THE ROLE OF GRACE IN FAITH AND BELIEVING

Faith and believing are essential components of the Christian life, yet both are deeply intertwined with the concept of divine grace. While believing can be seen as a human response to God's revelation, faith is more than a personal decision; it is a gift from God, granted through His grace. This chapter will explore how grace operates in both faith and believing, showing how divine grace enables us to believe and sustains our faith. We will delve into key biblical texts that illustrate the role of grace, with particular focus on Ephesians 2:8-9, which reminds us that faith is not our own doing, but a gift from God.

Faith as a Gift of Grace: Ephesians 2:8-9

Ephesians 2:8-9 is one of the foundational passages that illuminates the relationship between grace, faith, and salvation:

"For it is by grace you have been saved, through faith—and this is not from yourselves, it is the gift of God—not by works, so that no one can boast."

In this passage, Paul makes it clear that salvation comes through grace, which is mediated by faith. However, even the faith through which we are saved is not something we can generate on our own; it is a gift from God. Paul emphasizes that neither our faith nor our salvation is the result of human effort or merit. If it were, we could boast about our spiritual achievements. But because faith is a divine gift, it eliminates any grounds for pride.

Grace, in its simplest definition, is unmerited favor—God's goodness extended to humanity despite our unworthiness. When we speak of faith as a gift of grace, we recognize that our ability to believe, trust, and rely on God is not something we produce through our own strength or intellect. It is God who enables us to believe and sustain our faith. This understanding shifts the focus from human effort to divine initiative.

Grace Precedes Belief: The Role of God's Initiative

While belief often seems like an act of human will—our response to hearing the gospel—it is actually rooted in God's prior action of grace. Romans 10:17 says,

"So then faith comes by hearing, and hearing by the word of God."

Here, Paul acknowledges that faith arises from hearing God's word, but even hearing is an act of divine grace. God initiates the process of salvation by revealing Himself through His word, calling individuals to respond in belief. This revelation itself is an act of grace, as it opens our hearts and minds to the truth of the gospel. Without God's self-revelation, we would remain in spiritual darkness, unable to comprehend the truth.

Jesus Himself spoke of this divine initiative in John 6:44, where He said:

"No one can come to me unless the Father who sent me draws them, and I will raise them up at the last day."

This passage illustrates the role of God's grace in enabling belief. While belief is our response to the gospel, we can only come to faith because God, in His grace, draws us toward Himself. Our natural inclination, apart from God's grace, is to resist Him. Yet, by His grace, He opens our hearts to believe in the truth of Christ.

Belief and Grace: Human Response Empowered by Divine Grace

Belief, then, is not merely a cognitive or emotional decision, but a response that is empowered by God's grace. In Acts 16:14, we see an example of how God's grace works in the heart of an individual to enable belief:

"One of those listening was a woman from the city of Thyatira named Lydia, a dealer in purple cloth. She was a worshiper of God. The Lord opened her heart to respond to Paul's message."

This passage highlights a key aspect of belief: Lydia's heart was opened by the Lord. Although she was already a worshiper of God, it was God's grace that enabled her to truly believe in the gospel message that Paul preached. Her belief was not the result of mere intellectual persuasion but a work of grace that allowed her to embrace the truth.

In a similar way, every act of belief is grounded in the grace of God. When we come to faith, it is because God has opened our hearts and minds, allowing us to recognize the truth of the gospel. As we respond to God's call, His grace empowers our belief, turning it into something more than an intellectual decision—it becomes the beginning of a transformative relationship with Him.

The Role of Grace in Sustaining Faith

While grace initiates belief, it also sustains our faith throughout the Christian journey. The gift of faith is not a one-time event but an ongoing work of grace in the believer's life. Just as we cannot believe without God's grace, we cannot continue to live by faith without the continual support of His grace.

Philippians 1:6 assures us that:

"Being confident of this, that He who began a good work in you will carry it on to completion until the day of Christ Jesus."

This verse emphasizes that the same grace that initiated our faith will continue to sustain and perfect it. God is committed to nurturing the faith He has placed in us. As we face trials, doubts, and challenges in life, it is God's grace that strengthens our faith, allowing us to persevere and grow in our trust and reliance on Him.

Paul also recognized the ongoing role of grace in his own faith journey. In 2 Corinthians 12:9, he shares God's response to his plea for relief from a thorn in his flesh:

"But He said to me, 'My grace is sufficient for you, for my power is made perfect in weakness.' Therefore, I will boast all the more gladly about my weaknesses, so that Christ's power may rest on me."

In this passage, Paul acknowledges that it is God's grace that sustains him, especially in times of weakness. Paul's faith was not self-sustained; it was empowered by the grace of God, who provided the strength necessary for him to continue his ministry despite his challenges. This example reminds us that faith is not about human strength but about relying on the sufficiency of God's grace.

Grace, Faith, and Works: A Balanced Perspective

Understanding that faith is a gift of grace also helps us balance the relationship between faith and works. As we saw in James 2:14-26, true faith must be accompanied by works; however, these works are not the cause of salvation but the result of God's grace working in us.

Paul echoes this balance in Ephesians 2:10, which comes right after the well-known verses on grace and faith:

"For we are God's handiwork, created in Christ Jesus to do good works, which God prepared in advance for us to do."

While we are saved by grace through faith, the grace that saves us also empowers us to do the good works that God has planned for us. These works are not the basis of our salvation but are the natural outflow of a life transformed by grace. God's grace not only saves us but also equips and sustains us in living out our faith.

The Paradox of Grace and Human Responsibility

One of the mysteries of grace is how it interacts with human responsibility. While faith is a gift of grace, Scripture also calls us to believe, to trust, and to act in faith. This interplay between divine grace and human response can be difficult to fully comprehend, but the Bible presents them as complementary rather than contradictory.

Philippians 2:12-13 offers a helpful perspective:

"Therefore, my dear friends, as you have always obeyed—not only in my presence, but now much more in my absence—continue to work out your salvation with fear and trembling, for it is God who works in you to will and to act in order to fulfill His good purpose."

In this passage, Paul calls believers to "work out" their salvation, suggesting an active role in living out their faith. Yet, he immediately follows this by reminding them that it is God who works in them, both to will and to act according to His purposes. This demonstrates that while believers are called to respond in faith, it is God's grace that enables and sustains that response.

The Grace-Filled Nature of Faith and Believing

Faith is, at its core, a gift of grace. It is God's unmerited favor that enables us to believe in the truth of the gospel, to trust in His promises, and to live a life of faith. While belief may seem like a human response to God's revelation, even this act of belief is empowered by God's grace. As we come to faith, it is by grace that we are drawn to God, and it is by grace that our faith is sustained.

Understanding the role of grace in faith and believing reshapes how we view our relationship with God. It shifts the focus from our own efforts to the overwhelming generosity of God, who, by His grace, gives us the faith to trust in Him and sustains that faith throughout our lives. In the Christian life, grace and faith are inseparable. We believe because God has opened our hearts to His truth, and we continue to live by faith because His grace empowers us every step of the way.

Faith, then, is not something we can boast about, for it is not of ourselves—it is the gift of God, a work of His grace in us from beginning to end.

Supplements to Chapter 7: "The Role of Grace in Faith and Believing" Expository Bible Study and Commentary with Strong's Concordance

This chapter examines how grace operates as the divine foundation for faith and belief. Ephesians 2:8-9 emphasizes that faith is not a self-originated achievement but a gift of God's grace. Grace enables belief and empowers faith, positioning grace as the essential framework through which believers respond to God. This study will delve into key biblical passages that highlight the interaction between grace, faith, and belief, and how they work together to shape the Christian life.

Key Terms in Strong's Concordance

1. Grace (χάρις, charis) - Strong's G5485
2. Faith (πίστις, pistis) - Strong's G4102
3. Believe (πιστεύω, pisteuo) - Strong's G4100
4. Gift (δῶρον, doron) - Strong's G1435
5. Save (σῴζω, sozo) - Strong's G4982

Expository Bible Study and Commentary

Ephesians 2:8-9 - Saved by Grace Through Faith

"For by grace (charis - G5485) you have been saved (sozo - G4982) through faith (pistis - G4102), and that not of yourselves; it is the gift (doron - G1435) of God, not of works, lest anyone should boast."

- Strong's Analysis: "Grace" (charis - G5485) signifies favor or kindness freely given, while "faith" (pistis -

G4102) refers to trust and belief in God's promises. "Gift" (doron - G1435) here points to something granted unconditionally.

- Commentary: This passage asserts that salvation is solely by God's grace, received through faith, and independent of human effort. Grace precedes and enables faith, making it possible for believers to trust in Christ. Faith, therefore, is a response to God's grace, activated by divine initiative rather than human merit. The verse emphasizes that grace is the unearned gift of God, allowing no place for boasting, and underscores that true faith is a product of grace.

Romans 3:24-26 - Justified Freely by His Grace

"Being justified freely by His grace (charis - G5485) through the redemption that is in Christ Jesus, whom God set forth as a propitiation by His blood, through faith (pistis - G4102), to demonstrate His righteousness."

- Strong's Analysis: "Justified" refers to being declared righteous, a result of grace (charis - G5485), while "faith" (pistis - G4102) here signifies reliance on God's provision through Christ.

- Commentary: Paul explains that believers are justified (made right with God) freely by His grace. This grace is accessed through faith, showing that redemption is a gift made possible by God's initiative. Grace here is the means through which faith operates; without grace, there could be no faith. By focusing on God's act of redemption through Christ, Paul highlights that faith is inherently dependent on God's grace.

Titus 2:11 - Grace that Brings Salvation

"For the grace (charis - G5485) of God that brings salvation has appeared to all men."

- Strong's Analysis: The term "grace" (charis - G5485) denotes God's kindness and favor in offering salvation.

- Commentary: This passage reflects the universality of grace, indicating that God's grace offers salvation to all. While belief is the human acknowledgment of God's truth, grace is the divine provision that allows salvation to reach everyone. The passage points to the initiatory role of grace in the salvation experience, underscoring that belief is a response to this freely given grace.

John 1:16-17 - Grace and Truth Through Jesus Christ

"And of His fullness we have all received, and grace (charis - G5485) for grace. For the law was given through Moses, but grace and truth came through Jesus Christ."

- Strong's Analysis: "Grace" (charis - G5485) appears here as a successive, abundant gift, contrasted with the law.

- Commentary: John emphasizes that grace, as well as truth, is realized fully in Jesus Christ. While the law revealed humanity's need for a savior, grace fulfills that need. Through Christ, believers receive grace upon grace, an ongoing outpouring that continually empowers and sustains faith. This passage highlights the continual nature of grace, showing it as a sustaining power in the life of faith.

Romans 5:1-2 - Access to Grace by Faith

"Therefore, having been justified by faith (pistis - G4102), we have peace with God through our Lord Jesus Christ, through whom also we have access by faith into this grace in which we stand."

- Strong's Analysis: "Faith" (pistis - G4102) here is the means by which believers enter into and stand in "grace" (charis - G5485).

- Commentary: Paul explains that through faith, believers access the grace that justifies them before God. Grace is the sphere in which Christians "stand," and it is faith that enables entry into this divine favor. This grace brings reconciliation and peace with God, revealing faith as not just a starting point but a continued experience of God's grace. Paul's teaching reinforces the idea that while belief initiates the journey, faith continually engages and relies on grace.

Theological Insights on Grace, Faith, and Belief

1. Grace as the Source of Faith: Ephesians 2:8-9 underscores that faith is a gift of grace, affirming that faith does not originate from human effort but from God's initiative. Grace is the fertile ground from which faith grows, establishing that human belief alone cannot produce the kind of faith required for salvation. God's grace initiates faith, allowing believers to respond with trust and obedience.

2. Faith as the Response to Grace: In Romans 3:24-26, faith is portrayed as the human response to God's grace, specifically seen in His redemptive act through Christ. While belief accepts the truth of Christ's sacrifice, faith trusts in that sacrifice as the basis for justification. Faith, therefore, is more than acknowledgment; it is reliance upon grace.

3. Grace that Sustains Faith: John 1:16-17 and Romans 5:1-2 show that grace is not a one-time event but an ongoing reality that sustains and strengthens faith. Believers stand in grace continually, meaning that faith relies on God's unending grace to endure. Grace enables believers to grow from initial belief into mature, active faith, sustaining their relationship with God.

4. Faith and Works as Evidence of Grace: As seen in James 2, faith without works is dead; however, grace empowers believers to produce works that are evidence of true faith. Grace initiates, faith responds, and works manifest

as the outward expression of this divine interaction. True faith, originating in grace, naturally produces actions aligned with God's will.

Practical Applications of Grace in Faith and Believing

- Relying on Grace in Times of Doubt: When believers experience doubt or struggle, recalling that faith is a gift of grace can bring comfort and reassurance. Grace reassures that faith is sustained by God's initiative rather than human strength, encouraging believers to rely on God even in weakness.

- Praying for an Increase of Faith Through Grace: Recognizing that faith is a product of grace, believers can actively pray for an increase of faith, trusting that God will nurture and deepen it. Since faith originates in grace, prayer connects believers with God's continual outpouring of grace, helping faith to grow.

- Embracing Grace as the Foundation for Good Works: Understanding that faith is rooted in grace allows believers to engage in good works as a response to God's favor, not a way to earn it. This shifts the focus from performance to gratitude, as works become the natural outcome of a grace-filled faith.

- Acknowledging Dependence on God's Grace for Salvation: By recognizing that salvation is a gift, believers can let go of any sense of self-reliance and instead rest in the security of God's grace. This fosters humility, helping believers to understand that their faith is a divine gift, given freely and maintained by God's unmerited favor.

In summary, the Bible emphasizes that grace is foundational to both faith and belief. Grace initiates belief, sustains faith, and enables a living relationship with God. Faith, then, is a continual response to grace, expressed in trust, obedience, and works that honor God's provision. As believers grow in understanding of God's grace, their faith deepens, moving from belief into a vibrant, transformative relationship with God.

CHAPTER 08

FAITH IN PRACTICE: THE TRANSFORMATIONAL POWER OF TRUST

Faith is not just a theological concept or a mental agreement with truth—it is a lived experience that shapes every aspect of a Christian's life. When faith moves from mere belief to trust in God's promises, it transforms how we live, how we interact with others, and how we respond to life's challenges. Faith compels action, bringing about a life of obedience, reliance on God, and a heart that is continually renewed. This chapter will explore how faith is lived out in practice, drawing from biblical examples and offering practical ways to nurture and strengthen faith in everyday life.

The Hall of Faith: Hebrews 11

The "Hall of Faith" in Hebrews 11 serves as a powerful illustration of how faith compels action. This chapter lists numerous individuals who acted on their faith, trusting in God's promises even when circumstances seemed to contradict them. From Noah, who built an ark when there was no sign of rain, to Abraham, who left his homeland without knowing where he was going, the people mentioned in Hebrews 11 exemplify faith in practice.

Hebrews 11:1 begins with a profound definition of faith:

"Now faith is confidence in what we hope for and assurance about what we do not see."

Faith is not dependent on what is visible or immediately attainable. It is a confidence in the promises of God, even when those promises have yet to be fulfilled. The individuals in Hebrews 11 acted on their faith, trusting God's word despite uncertainty, danger, or hardship.

For example, Hebrews 11:7 highlights Noah's faith:

"By faith Noah, when warned about things not yet seen, in holy fear built an ark to save his family. By his faith he condemned the world and became heir of the righteousness that is in keeping with faith."

Noah's faith was not passive; it required action. He believed God's warning about the coming flood and acted in obedience, building the ark as a tangible expression of his trust in God's word. This kind of faith transforms not only the individual but also the community, as Noah's faith saved his family and preserved humanity.

Similarly, Abraham's faith was marked by radical trust in God's promises, even when those promises seemed impossible. Hebrews 11:8 recounts:

"By faith Abraham, when called to go to a place he would later receive as his inheritance, obeyed and went, even though he did not know where he was going."

Abraham's faith led him to leave behind everything familiar, trusting that God would guide him to the promised land. His faith was demonstrated through obedience, even in the face of uncertainty. Faith in practice, as these examples show, is not merely intellectual belief; it involves trust in God's promises and a willingness to act in accordance with His will.

Obedience: Faith in Action

One of the clearest ways that faith manifests itself in the life of a Christian is through obedience. When we trust in God, we naturally seek to align our actions with His will, even when it may be difficult or counterintuitive. Jesus Himself emphasized the connection between faith and obedience in John 14:15, where He said:

"If you love me, keep my commands."

Faith and love for God are evidenced by our willingness to follow His commands. Obedience is not about earning God's favor but about demonstrating our trust in His goodness and wisdom. When we have faith in God's character, we are more likely to obey, knowing that His ways are higher than ours and that His commands are for our ultimate good.

Consider the example of Peter walking on water in Matthew 14:28-31. When Peter saw Jesus walking on the water, he asked to join Him. Jesus told him to come, and Peter stepped out of the boat in faith. As long as Peter kept his eyes on Jesus, he was able to walk on the water. But when he became distracted by the wind and waves, he began to sink. This story highlights the importance of obedience in faith. Peter's faith allowed him to step out in trust, but his faith faltered when he took his focus off Jesus.

Faith in practice requires both trust and obedience, even when circumstances seem overwhelming. Obedience to God's word is the outward expression of our inward faith, showing that we trust in His promises and His guidance.

Faith Transforms the Heart

Faith not only leads to external actions but also transforms the heart. When we place our trust in God, He begins a work of transformation within us, molding our hearts to reflect His character. This transformation is a key aspect of faith in practice.

Romans 12:2 encourages believers:

"Do not conform to the pattern of this world, but be transformed by the renewing of your mind. Then you will be able to test and approve what God's will is—His good, pleasing and perfect will."

Faith allows us to be renewed, both in mind and heart, as we trust in God's ability to change us from the inside out. This transformation is not a one-time event but an ongoing process of sanctification, where our desires, thoughts, and actions are increasingly aligned with God's will.

Faith in practice involves surrendering our will to God and allowing Him to shape us. This transformation is often seen in the fruit of the Spirit, described in Galatians 5:22-23:

"But the fruit of the Spirit is love, joy, peace, forbearance, kindness, goodness, faithfulness, gentleness, and self-control."

As our faith deepens, the Holy Spirit works within us to produce these qualities, transforming our character to reflect Christ. Faith changes not only how we act but also who we are at the core, making us more loving, patient, and faithful people.

Nurturing Faith Through Prayer, Scripture, and Community

Faith, like any other aspect of spiritual life, needs to be nurtured and strengthened. While faith is a gift from God, we have a role to play in cultivating it. Three key practices help nurture faith in the life of a believer: prayer, scripture, and community.

1. Prayer:

Prayer is the lifeblood of faith. Through prayer, we communicate with God, bringing our fears, doubts, and requests before Him while also listening for His guidance. Philippians 4:6-7 encourages us to pray in faith, trusting that God will provide peace:

"Do not be anxious about anything, but in every situation, by prayer and petition, with thanksgiving, present your requests to God. And the peace of God, which transcends all understanding, will guard your hearts and your minds in Christ Jesus."

Regular prayer strengthens our faith by deepening our relationship with God and reminding us of His constant presence. As we pray, we grow in our trust that God hears and answers our prayers according to His perfect will.

2. Scripture:

God's word is foundational to building faith. Romans 10:17 tells us that:

"Faith comes from hearing the message, and the message is heard through the word about Christ."

Immersing ourselves in Scripture strengthens our faith by reminding us of God's promises, His character, and His faithfulness throughout history. The Bible is full of examples of how God has acted in the lives of His people, and by studying it, we learn to trust Him more deeply. Regular engagement with Scripture equips us to live out our faith in practical ways, providing wisdom and guidance for our daily lives.

3. Community:

Faith is not meant to be lived out in isolation. Christian community provides support, encouragement, and accountability. Hebrews 10:24-25 emphasizes the importance of fellowship in nurturing faith:

"And let us consider how we may spur one another on toward love and good deeds, not giving up meeting together, as some are in the habit of doing, but encouraging one another—and all the more as you see the Day approaching."

Being part of a community of believers helps strengthen our faith as we share our experiences, pray for one another, and encourage each other to trust in God. Community provides a space for us to practice faith together, learning from one another's struggles and triumphs in living out our trust in God.

Faith in the Midst of Trials

Faith is often most clearly seen in times of trial. When life is difficult, and circumstances seem overwhelming, faith calls us to trust in God's promises, even when we cannot see the outcome. 1 Peter 1:6-7 reminds us that trials are opportunities for our faith to be refined:

"In all this you greatly rejoice, though now for a little while you may have had to suffer grief in all kinds of trials. These have come so that the proven genuineness of your faith—of greater worth than gold, which perishes even though refined by fire—may result in praise, glory, and honor when Jesus Christ is revealed."

Faith is not a guarantee of an easy life, but it is the assurance that God is with us, even in the hardest times. As we trust Him through trials, our faith is strengthened, and our relationship with Him deepens. Faith transforms suffering into an opportunity for growth, as we learn to rely on God's strength rather than our own.

Faith That Transforms

Faith is more than an abstract belief; it is a lived experience that transforms every aspect of the Christian's life. It compels us to act in obedience to God's will, leads to the transformation of our hearts, and sustains us through trials. Faith is both a gift from God and a responsibility we must nurture through prayer, Scripture, and community.

As we grow in faith, we begin to see the world through the lens of trust in God's promises. Our lives become marked by a deep reliance on God, a commitment to His will, and a confidence that He is working all things together for our good. Faith in practice is transformational, shaping who we are, how we live, and how we relate to the world around us. Through faith, we are empowered to live lives that reflect the love, grace, and power of the God we trust.

Supplements to Chapter 8: "Faith in Practice: The Transformational Power of Trust" Expository Bible Study and Commentary with Strong's Concordance

This chapter addresses how living out faith translates into a transformed life marked by trust, obedience, and a strengthened relationship with God. Faith in practice is more than an intellectual belief or passive acceptance; it is an active, lived commitment to God. Hebrews 11, known as the "Hall of Faith," presents individuals who practiced their faith by acting on God's promises despite obstacles, showcasing the deep, transformative power of trust in God.

Key Terms in Strong's Concordance

1. Faith (πίστις, pistis) - Strong's G4102

2. Trust (ἐλπίζω, elpizo) - Strong's G1679

3. Obey (ὑπακούω, hupakouo) - Strong's G5219

4. Action/Work (ἔργον, ergon) - Strong's G2041

5. Transformation (μεταμορφόω, metamorphoo) - Strong's G3339

Expository Bible Study and Commentary

Hebrews 11:1 - Faith as Assurance and Conviction

"Now faith (pistis - G4102) is the assurance of things hoped for, the conviction of things not seen."

- Strong's Analysis: "Faith" (pistis - G4102) is defined as both "assurance" and "conviction," portraying faith as deeply rooted in trust and confidence in God's promises.

- Commentary: Hebrews 11:1 provides a foundational definition of faith, describing it as an active assurance in what is hoped for and a firm conviction in the unseen. This faith is not passive but shapes the believer's reality and response to God. The verse positions faith as transformative, guiding believers to trust God even without visible evidence. This form of faith is instrumental in practicing trust, showing that it involves confident reliance on God's character and promises.

James 2:17 - Faith Without Works is Dead

"Thus also faith (pistis - G4102) by itself, if it does not have works (ergon - G2041), is dead."

- Strong's Analysis: "Works" (ergon - G2041) signifies actions or deeds that reveal the sincerity of faith.

- Commentary: James emphasizes that genuine faith naturally produces works as its evidence. Faith in practice means that beliefs must be backed by actions, confirming the inner transformation that faith brings. This is essential in showing that faith is more than intellectual assent; it is a commitment to live according to God's will, demonstrated through obedience, service, and moral integrity. James's message encourages believers to actively embody faith, expressing it through practical deeds that impact others.

Romans 12:2 - Transformation by the Renewal of the Mind

"And do not be conformed to this world, but be transformed (metamorphoo - G3339) by the renewal of your mind, that you may prove what is that good and acceptable and perfect will of God."

- Strong's Analysis: "Transformed" (metamorphoo - G3339) reflects a change in form or character, often associated with a profound inner transformation.

- Commentary: Paul's exhortation in Romans highlights the role of faith in transforming believers' lives by renewing their minds and aligning them with God's will. Faith in practice renews perspectives, changes attitudes, and motivates behavior. This transformation occurs as believers trust and obey God, leading them to reflect His character. The call to be "transformed" signifies a fundamental shift from self-centeredness to a life grounded in God's purposes, underscoring how faith shapes one's entire identity and outlook.

Proverbs 3:5-6 - Trust in the Lord

"Trust (batach - H982) in the LORD with all your heart, and lean not on your own understanding; in all your ways acknowledge Him, and He shall direct your paths."

- Strong's Analysis: "Trust" (batach - H982) means to have confidence or reliance on God.

- Commentary: This passage underscores the essence of faith as trust in God, calling believers to depend on Him rather than their understanding. Faith in practice is marked by surrender to God's guidance, allowing Him to direct life's path. True trust is a demonstration of faith that seeks God's will, showing a reliance that transcends human reasoning. Proverbs 3:5-6 illustrates that practical faith leads to a guided and purposeful life, with each step taken in alignment with God's will.

Matthew 7:24-25 - Faith as Building on the Rock

"Therefore, everyone who hears these words of Mine, and acts on them, will be like a wise man who built his house on the rock."

- Strong's Analysis: "Acts" (poieo - G4160) emphasizes taking deliberate action based on Jesus' teachings.

- Commentary: Jesus likens faith in practice to building a house on a solid foundation, reflecting obedience to His words. Faith transforms by leading believers to trust in the foundation of Christ's teachings and live accordingly. The emphasis on acting (poieo) demonstrates that true faith requires more than hearing; it demands application. This analogy reveals that faith endures life's storms because it is grounded in a secure, unshakable trust in God's truth.

Theological Insights on Faith as Transformative Trust

1. Faith as an Active Trust in God's Promises: Hebrews 11 portrays faith as reliance on God's promises, producing confidence and resilience in trials. Practical faith does not simply accept beliefs but lives by them, trusting God's promises as though they are fulfilled.

2. Transformation Through Obedience: Romans 12:2 illustrates that transformation through faith involves a shift from worldly influences toward a life marked by godly principles. The renewing of the mind aligns believers with

God's values, showing that faith practiced daily creates a transformation reflecting God's character.

3. Works as the Natural Expression of Faith: James 2 establishes that true faith results in works, underscoring the inseparable link between faith and action. Faith that remains unexpressed is incomplete; genuine faith naturally overflows in actions that impact others and reflect obedience to God.

4. Trust in God Over Self: Proverbs 3:5-6 highlights that faith is trusting God's wisdom over one's understanding. Faith, therefore, is not passive reliance but active surrender, depending on God's direction and entrusting every aspect of life to His care. This complete reliance signifies the depth of transformative trust.

5. Building a Life on Christ's Teachings: Matthew 7 emphasizes that faith in action means grounding one's life on Jesus' teachings, with trust as the foundation. Faith that transforms is like building on rock, reflecting that the strength of faith is proven through obedience and application of God's Word.

Practical Applications of Faith as Transformational Trust

- Daily Surrender to God's Will: Faith in practice requires daily surrender to God's will, trusting Him in decisions, relationships, and personal challenges. By acknowledging God in all areas, believers cultivate a deep reliance on His wisdom, moving beyond intellectual belief to a lived trust.

- Consistency in Spiritual Disciplines: Developing a disciplined prayer life, studying scripture, and engaging with a community of faith reinforces trust in God and strengthens one's foundation in faith. These disciplines align believers with God's presence, providing a steady source of strength and guidance.

- Acting in Faith Despite Uncertainty: Trusting God often requires action despite fear or doubt. Faith in practice compels believers to act in obedience, even when circumstances are uncertain, allowing God's promises to shape decisions and responses.

- Serving Others as an Expression of Faith: Faith that transforms leads believers to serve others selflessly. Acts of kindness, generosity, and compassion are ways that faith is expressed in practical life, reflecting God's love and impacting the world positively.

Faith in practice, as demonstrated by trust and obedience, results in a life continually shaped and transformed by God's presence and promises. Through the examples of Hebrews 11 and other scriptural insights, believers see that faith is more than belief; it is an enduring trust that reshapes their thoughts, actions, and character, embodying a transformative power that deepens their relationship with God and reveals His grace through their lives.

CHAPTER 09

FAITH, WORKS, AND BELIEF: CLARIFYING MISCONCEPTIONS

The relationship between faith, works, and belief has been a topic of theological discussion for centuries. While some argue that faith alone is sufficient for salvation, others emphasize the importance of works in demonstrating faith. Both Scripture and Christian tradition provide a balanced view, but misunderstandings often arise when these elements are separated or overemphasized. This chapter will explore the dynamic interplay between faith, works, and belief by examining key biblical texts, such as James 2 and Ephesians 2, and addressing common misconceptions about their relationship.

Faith and Belief: Understanding the Distinction

Before diving into the role of works, it is essential to clarify the distinction between faith and belief. As discussed in previous chapters, belief refers to the intellectual acceptance of certain truths, such as the existence of God or the divinity of Christ. Belief is foundational, as it acknowledges the truth of the gospel, but belief alone is insufficient for salvation.

James 2:19 offers a stark warning:

"You believe that there is one God. Good! Even the demons believe that—and shudder."

This passage highlights that belief, while necessary, is not enough to save. Even the demons believe in God's existence, but their belief does not lead to salvation or obedience. Belief must be accompanied by faith, which involves trust, commitment, and reliance on God. Faith goes beyond mere intellectual assent and transforms belief into a lived, relational trust in God's promises.

Faith Alone Saves: Ephesians 2:8-9

One of the central passages used to emphasize that faith alone saves is Ephesians 2:8-9:

"For it is by grace you have been saved, through faith—and this is not from yourselves, it is the gift of God—not by works, so that no one can boast."

In this passage, Paul makes it clear that salvation is a gift of grace, accessed through faith. Works cannot earn salvation, nor can human effort merit God's favor. Salvation is entirely the result of God's grace, and faith is the means by which we receive that grace. This is the essence of the doctrine of sola fide ("faith alone"), a foundational principle of Protestant theology that asserts that salvation is through faith, not works.

However, this passage does not diminish the importance of works. Instead, it highlights that works are not the cause of salvation, but the result. Works flow from the grace we have received through faith. They are the evidence of faith, not the basis of salvation. Ephesians 2:10, the verse immediately following Paul's assertion of salvation by grace through faith, reinforces this:

"For we are God's handiwork, created in Christ Jesus to do good works, which God prepared in advance for us to do."

This verse shows that good works are a vital part of the Christian life, not as a means to earn salvation, but as a natural outflow of a life transformed by God's grace. Faith, when genuine, produces good works as evidence of its authenticity.

Faith Without Works Is Dead: James 2

While Paul emphasizes the primacy of faith for salvation, James offers a complementary perspective on the relationship between faith and works. James 2:14-17 challenges the notion that faith can exist without works:

"What good is it, my brothers and sisters, if someone claims to have faith but has no deeds? Can such faith save them? Suppose a brother or a sister is without clothes and daily food. If one of you says to them, 'Go in peace; keep warm and well fed,' but does nothing about their physical needs, what good is it? In the same way, faith by itself, if it is not accompanied by action, is dead."

James is not contradicting Paul's teaching on salvation by faith alone. Instead, he is addressing a different issue: the misconception that intellectual belief alone is sufficient for salvation. James argues that faith, if genuine, will naturally result in works. Works are the visible evidence that faith is alive and active. If faith does not lead to tangible acts of love, charity, and obedience, then it is not true faith, but a lifeless form of belief.

James further strengthens this argument by referring to the example of Abraham. In James 2:21-22, he writes:

"Was not our father Abraham considered righteous for what he did when he offered his son Isaac on the altar? You see that his faith and his actions were working together, and his faith was made complete by what he did."

Abraham's willingness to sacrifice Isaac was not the cause of his righteousness, but the demonstration of his faith.

His works validated and completed his faith, showing that his trust in God was real. James concludes this section by stating,

"As the body without the spirit is dead, so faith without deeds is dead." (James 2:26).

James' message is clear: faith without works is incomplete and ineffective. Genuine faith results in action, not as a means of earning salvation, but as the natural fruit of a heart transformed by God's grace.

Clarifying the Misconceptions

The perceived tension between Paul's teaching on faith and James' emphasis on works has led to various misconceptions. Some have interpreted Paul's assertion that we are saved by grace through faith as a rejection of the importance of works, leading to the belief that actions or obedience are unnecessary for a life of faith. Others have overemphasized James' teaching, leading to a works-based view of salvation.

The truth, as Scripture reveals, is that faith and works are not in opposition but are complementary. Here are some key points that clarify common misconceptions:

1. Faith Alone Saves, but Saving Faith Is Never Alone:

Paul's teaching in Ephesians 2:8-9 establishes that salvation is by faith alone, not by works. However, this faith is never "alone" in the sense of being inactive. True faith always produces good works, as Ephesians 2:10 and James 2 demonstrate. Works are the fruit of faith, not the root of salvation. When we are saved by grace, our faith naturally leads to a life of obedience and good deeds.

2. Works Are a Response to Grace, Not a Means of Earning It:

Works are an essential part of the Christian life, but they are not the means by which we earn God's favor. Instead, they are a response to the grace we have already received. As Titus 3:5 reminds us:

"He saved us, not because of righteous things we had done, but because of His mercy."

Works flow from a heart of gratitude and a desire to honor God, not from a desire to earn His favor. They are the evidence of a transformed life, not the basis of salvation.

3. Faith and Works Are Interconnected:

Both Paul and James agree that faith and works are interconnected. While Paul emphasizes the role of faith in justification, he also acknowledges the necessity of good works as the outworking of that faith. Similarly, while James highlights the importance of works, he does not deny the foundational role of faith in salvation. Both apostles teach that genuine faith results in works, and true works are rooted in faith.

4. Belief Must Lead to Trust and Obedience:

Intellectual belief, while necessary, is not sufficient for salvation. Faith must go beyond belief and result in trust, reliance, and obedience to God's commands. This is why James warns against the danger of a faith that consists only of mental assent without corresponding action. True faith transforms belief into a living, active trust in God.

Faith and Works in Jesus' Teachings

Jesus Himself emphasized the importance of both faith and works in the life of a believer. In Matthew 7:21, Jesus says:

"Not everyone who says to me, 'Lord, Lord,' will enter the kingdom of heaven, but only the one who does the will of my Father who is in heaven."

This statement highlights that mere verbal acknowledgment of Jesus as Lord—intellectual belief—is not enough. True faith is evidenced by doing the will of God, which involves obedience and action. Jesus' parables, such as the parable of the Good Samaritan, further illustrate that faith must result in love, compassion, and service to others.

In John 14:12, Jesus also emphasizes the role of works in the life of those who have faith in Him:

"Very truly I tell you, whoever believes in me will do the works I have been doing, and they will do even greater things than these, because I am going to the Father."

Faith in Jesus naturally leads to works that reflect His character and mission. Just as Jesus' ministry was marked by acts of love, healing, and compassion, so too are His followers called to live out their faith through similar acts of service and obedience.

The Balanced Relationship Between Faith, Works, and Belief

The relationship between faith, works, and belief is not one of competition or contradiction, but of harmony. Belief is essential, but it must lead to faith, which in turn produces works. Faith alone saves, as Paul teaches, but as James emphasizes, faith that does not result in works is dead. Works are the natural outflow of a heart transformed by grace and a life lived in faith.

As believers, we are called to embrace the fullness of this relationship, recognizing that while our salvation is secured by grace through faith, our faith is made complete by our actions. Works do not earn salvation, but they reveal the authenticity of our faith and demonstrate the power of God's grace at work in our lives.

Supplements to Chapter 9: "Faith, Works, and Belief: Clarifying Misconceptions"

Expository Bible Study and Commentary with Strong's Concordance

This chapter aims to clarify misconceptions surrounding the interplay of faith, works, and belief, particularly addressing the relationship between faith alone and faith demonstrated through works. Key passages such as James 2 and Ephesians 2 often generate discussion on whether salvation comes through faith alone or through a combination of faith and works. Understanding these scriptural nuances helps us grasp how faith, works, and belief complement each other in the life of a Christian.

Key Terms in Strong's Concordance

1. Faith (πίστις, pistis) - Strong's G4102

2. Works (ἔργον, ergon) - Strong's G2041

3. Believe (πιστεύω, pisteuo) - Strong's G4100

4. Grace (χάρις, charis) - Strong's G5485

5. Saved (σῴζω, sozo) - Strong's G4982

Expository Bible Study and Commentary

Ephesians 2:8-9 – Salvation by Grace Through Faith

"For by grace (charis - G5485) you have been saved (sozo - G4982) through faith (pistis - G4102), and that not of yourselves; it is the gift of God, not of works (ergon - G2041), lest anyone should boast."

- Strong's Analysis: "Grace" (charis - G5485) signifies God's unmerited favor, while "saved" (sozo - G4982) refers to deliverance or preservation, emphasizing that salvation is a divine gift rather than human achievement.

- Commentary: This passage emphasizes that salvation is a gift received through faith, not earned through works. Paul explains that grace is foundational to salvation, highlighting that faith alone allows individuals to receive this grace. This verse clarifies that works cannot earn or secure salvation; rather, they are a response to the grace received. Understanding salvation as a gift prevents boasting and reaffirms the centrality of faith, underscoring God's role in the believer's life.

James 2:14-17 – Faith Without Works is Dead

"What does it profit, my brethren, if someone says he has faith but does not have works? Can faith save him? ... Thus also faith (pistis - G4102) by itself, if it does not have works (ergon - G2041), is dead."

- Strong's Analysis: "Works" (ergon - G2041) refers to deeds or actions, indicating tangible demonstrations of inner faith.

- Commentary: James emphasizes that true faith is evidenced by works, affirming that a faith without corresponding actions is ineffective or "dead." Here, James is not arguing against salvation by faith alone but rather insisting that genuine faith produces a lifestyle aligned with God's will. This passage shows that works reveal the authenticity of faith and make it complete. Faith without action is inactive and unproductive, lacking the power to influence or transform, which James critiques as incomplete.

Galatians 2:16 – Justified by Faith, Not by Works of the Law

"Knowing that a man is not justified by the works of the law but by faith (pistis - G4102) in Jesus Christ, even we have believed (pisteuo - G4100) in Christ Jesus, that we might be justified by faith in Christ and not by the works of the law; for by the works of the law no flesh shall be justified."

- Strong's Analysis: "Justified" (dikaioo - G1344) means to be declared righteous, and "works of the law" implies the observance of Mosaic Law as a basis for righteousness.

- Commentary: Paul's emphasis on justification through faith rather than works of the law clarifies that righteousness before God is not earned through human efforts but is granted by faith in Jesus Christ. This verse addresses Jewish Christians who relied on the law for justification, contrasting legalistic works with a faith-centered relationship with God. Paul's message highlights that faith in Christ is the only way to receive righteousness, and works of the law cannot replace or equal the righteousness received through faith.

Titus 3:8 – The Role of Good Works as a Response to Faith

"This is a faithful saying, and these things I want you to affirm constantly, that those who have believed (pisteuo - G4100) in God should be careful to maintain good works (ergon - G2041). These things are good and profitable to men."

- Strong's Analysis: "Maintain" (proistemi - G4291) suggests a continuous effort, indicating that believers are called to regularly engage in good works.

- Commentary: Titus underscores that while salvation is by faith, good works remain integral to the Christian life. Paul encourages believers to be devoted to good works, not as a means of achieving salvation but as an expression of their faith. These works are "good and profitable," implying that they bless others and reinforce the believer's witness. Thus, good works complement faith, showcasing its genuine nature and benefiting the community.

Romans 3:28 – Justification by Faith Apart from the Law

"Therefore we conclude that a man is justified by faith (pistis - G4102) apart from the deeds (ergon - G2041) of the law."

- Strong's Analysis: "Apart from" (choris - G5565) indicates independence, showing that justification through faith stands independently of the law.

- Commentary: Paul reaffirms the doctrine of justification by faith, independent of the law, emphasizing that legalistic deeds cannot justify. This verse, similar to Galatians 2:16, stresses that salvation is based solely on faith in Christ, not on one's adherence to religious rules. Justification by faith eliminates the requirement for external actions to earn salvation, highlighting that faith alone positions believers in a right relationship with God.

Theological Insights on Faith, Works, and Belief

1. Faith as the Foundation of Salvation: Ephesians 2:8-9 and Romans 3:28 affirm that faith is the sole means of receiving salvation. This belief underscores God's grace as the cornerstone of salvation, accessible only through faith, and not by works. Faith, therefore, forms the starting point and basis of a believer's relationship with God.

2. Works as Evidence of Faith: James 2 teaches that works reveal the presence and vitality of faith. Works do not

replace faith but express it, validating the believer's internal transformation. Genuine faith naturally leads to works, as they reflect an active trust in God.

3. The Harmony Between Faith and Works: Although Paul emphasizes justification by faith alone, he also acknowledges in passages like Titus 3:8 that good works are the fruit of a believer's life. Works are the practical manifestation of a faith that saves, highlighting that a genuine faith is visible and impactful.

4. Grace as the Source of Justification: Titus 3:8 and Galatians 2:16 confirm that grace, not human merit, is the basis for justification. This grace is accessed through faith and is evidenced by works. Grace makes possible what human efforts cannot achieve—right standing before God and the ability to live in harmony with His will.

Practical Applications of Faith, Works, and Belief

- Living Out Faith Through Action: James encourages believers to put their faith into practice, demonstrating it through actions that serve others. Practicing faith in everyday life provides a witness to others and strengthens the believer's commitment to God's purposes.

- Balancing Faith and Works: Christians should understand works as an outgrowth of faith, not a means of earning God's favor. Believers can cultivate good works as a response to salvation, serving others out of love and gratitude.

- Trusting in God's Grace Over Human Effort: Recognizing that salvation is a gift allows believers to rely on God's grace rather than personal achievements. This trust in grace fosters a deeper sense of humility and gratitude, encouraging believers to serve out of love rather than obligation.

- Maintaining Good Works as a Testimony: Titus reminds Christians to engage in good works consistently, not for self-righteousness but as a reflection of their faith. By maintaining a lifestyle of service and compassion, believers showcase the reality of their faith to others, embodying God's love.

Summary

The relationship between faith, works, and belief is one of balance and harmony. Faith, as the foundation of salvation, comes through grace alone, and works are the natural outcome of a living faith. True faith in Christ, as shown in the scriptures, does not exist without evidence in action. Faith justifies and secures the believer's salvation, while works give evidence to the transformative power of that faith. This perspective aligns believers with God's purposes, ensuring that their faith is not passive but alive and active in demonstrating God's love to others.

CHAPTER 10

FAITH AND SALVATION: A GIFT BEYOND BELIEF

Salvation is the cornerstone of Christian doctrine, and it is often described as a gift of grace received through faith. While belief plays a crucial role in salvation, it is faith—an active trust and reliance on God—that brings this gift into reality. Faith goes beyond intellectual acknowledgment of God's existence or the truth of the gospel; it is a transformative experience that affects the heart, mind, and soul. In this chapter, we will explore how salvation is realized through faith in Jesus Christ, examine the deeper meaning of faith in the context of salvation, and address common questions regarding the role of faith and belief in receiving this divine gift.

Salvation by Grace Through Faith: Ephesians 2:8-9

The Apostle Paul's teaching in Ephesians 2:8-9 offers a foundational understanding of salvation:

"For it is by grace you have been saved, through faith—and this is not from yourselves, it is the gift of God—not by works, so that no one can boast."

In this passage, Paul emphasizes that salvation is entirely the work of God's grace. It is not something we can earn or achieve through human effort or good works. Instead, salvation is a gift, freely given to us by God, and received through faith. This is a critical distinction: grace is the means of salvation, and faith is the channel through which we access that grace.

This passage also underscores the humility required to receive salvation. Since it is "not by works," no one can boast about their own spiritual achievements. Salvation is not something we can take credit for; it is entirely dependent on God's gracious initiative and our response of faith.

The Role of Belief in Salvation

Belief is an essential first step in the process of salvation. John 3:16, one of the most well-known verses in the Bible, stresses the importance of belief:

"For God so loved the world that He gave His one and only Son, that whoever believes in Him shall not perish but have eternal life."

Believing in Jesus Christ as the Son of God and Savior is necessary for salvation. This belief acknowledges the truth of the gospel—that Jesus lived, died, and rose again to save us from sin. However, belief alone is not enough. As we have seen in earlier chapters, even the demons believe in God's existence (James 2:19), but their belief does not lead to salvation. Belief, while crucial, must be accompanied by faith—a trust that leads to transformation and action.

Romans 10:9 further explains the connection between belief and salvation:

"If you declare with your mouth, 'Jesus is Lord,' and believe in your heart that God raised him from the dead, you will be saved."

Here, belief is linked with confession and faith in action. It is not merely a mental acknowledgment of Jesus' identity but a heartfelt conviction that leads to the surrender of one's life to Him. This belief opens the door to salvation, but it is faith that carries us through, transforming us into new creations in Christ.

Faith: The Transformative Element of Salvation

Faith, in the context of salvation, goes beyond simple belief. It is an all-encompassing trust in Jesus Christ as both Savior and Lord. This faith transforms the believer's heart, mind, and soul. It leads to a personal relationship with God, one that changes the way we live, think, and interact with the world.

When we place our faith in Jesus, we are not merely accepting Him as a historical figure or acknowledging His divinity. Instead, we are entrusting our entire lives to Him. This act of faith involves turning away from sin, surrendering our will to God, and living in alignment with His purposes.

2 Corinthians 5:17 describes the transformation that occurs when faith brings salvation into reality:

"Therefore, if anyone is in Christ, the new creation has come: The old has gone, the new is here!"

This transformation is not just a change in behavior but a profound spiritual rebirth. Through faith, we are made new in Christ. Our sins are forgiven, our hearts are changed, and we are given the Holy Spirit to guide and empower us in our walk with God.

Faith is not a one-time event but an ongoing relationship with God. As we grow in faith, we experience continual transformation, becoming more like Christ in our thoughts, actions, and character. This is the essence of salvation: not merely escaping the penalty of sin, but being made new, restored to a right relationship with God, and empowered to live out our faith in practical ways.

Faith as Trust in Jesus Christ

At the core of saving faith is trust in Jesus Christ. This trust is not abstract or theoretical; it is deeply personal. It involves placing our hope and confidence in Christ's finished work on the cross and His resurrection from the dead. It means trusting that His sacrifice is sufficient to cover our sins and reconcile us to God.

Acts 16:31 captures the simplicity and depth of this trust:

"Believe in the Lord Jesus, and you will be saved—you and your household."

This trust is both the beginning of the Christian life and the foundation for everything that follows. When we trust in Jesus, we are acknowledging that we cannot save ourselves and that we need His grace and mercy. This trust moves us from self-reliance to reliance on God, from pride to humility, and from death to life.

Faith in Christ is what allows us to experience the fullness of salvation. It is through faith that we receive forgiveness, justification, and adoption into God's family. Trusting in Jesus means we are confident that His promises are true and that He is faithful to complete the work He has begun in us.

Common Questions About Faith and Salvation

As we explore the relationship between faith and salvation, several common questions arise. Understanding these questions helps clarify the nature of salvation and the role of faith in receiving it.

1. Is Belief Enough for Salvation?

As we've discussed, belief is necessary for salvation but not sufficient on its own. Belief must lead to faith, which involves trust, commitment, and transformation. Intellectual acknowledgment of the gospel is not enough; salvation requires a heart-level trust in Jesus Christ and a willingness to follow Him.

2. Can Faith Be Lost?

This is a deeply debated question in Christian theology, and views vary. Some traditions hold that salvation, once received, cannot be lost because it is a work of God's grace. Others believe that persistent unbelief or rebellion can lead a person to fall away from faith. What is clear from Scripture is that those who have genuine faith will persevere, not by their own strength, but by the sustaining grace of God. Philippians 1:6 offers comfort:

"He who began a good work in you will carry it on to completion until the day of Christ Jesus."

3. What Is the Role of Works in Salvation?

As discussed in earlier chapters, works do not contribute to our salvation, but they are the fruit of genuine faith. James 2:26 reminds us:

"As the body without the spirit is dead, so faith without deeds is dead."

Works are the evidence of a living faith. They do not save us, but they demonstrate the reality of our salvation. Faith that does not result in a transformed life and good works is incomplete and not truly saving faith.

4. Is Salvation Instantaneous or a Process?

Salvation is both an event and a process. It is instantaneous in the sense that, when we place our faith in Christ, we are justified—declared righteous before God. This happens at the moment of belief. However, salvation is also a process, known as sanctification, in which we grow in holiness and become more like Christ over time. This process continues throughout the believer's life and is completed when we are finally glorified in God's presence.

The Assurance of Salvation Through Faith

One of the most profound gifts of faith is the assurance of salvation. When we trust in Christ, we can be confident that our salvation is secure, not because of our own efforts but because of God's faithfulness. 1 John 5:13 offers this assurance:

"I write these things to you who believe in the name of the Son of God so that you may know that you have eternal life."

This assurance is not based on our feelings or performance but on the promises of God. Through faith, we can know that we are saved, that our sins are forgiven, and that we have eternal life in Christ. This confidence allows us to live with peace and joy, knowing that nothing can separate us from the love of God in Christ Jesus (Romans 8:38-39).

Faith as the Key to Salvation

Salvation, according to Christian doctrine, is a gift of grace, accessed through faith. Belief in the gospel is essential, but faith is what brings salvation into reality. Faith goes beyond intellectual assent; it involves a transformation of the heart, mind, and soul, leading to a personal relationship with Jesus Christ.

As we place our trust in Christ, we experience the fullness of salvation—justification, sanctification, and the promise of eternal life. Faith is not static; it grows and deepens as we continue to trust in God's promises and live out our faith in obedience to His will.

Ultimately, faith is the key that unlocks the gift of salvation. It is through faith that we receive the grace of God, and it is through faith that we are continually transformed into the image of Christ. As we trust in Him, we are given the assurance of salvation, the joy of a transformed life, and the hope of eternal life with God.

Supplements to Chapter 10: "Faith and Salvation: A Gift Beyond Belief" Expository

Bible Study and Commentary with Strong's Concordance

In this chapter, we explore the relationship between faith, belief, and salvation. Ephesians 2:8-9 emphasizes that salvation is a divine gift given by God's grace and received through faith. While belief in the truths of the gospel is crucial, faith goes beyond mere mental assent—it involves a transformation that aligns with salvation. This chapter focuses on the distinctive elements of faith that make salvation a reality and how this faith is God's gift rather than a human achievement.

Key Terms in Strong's Concordance

1. Faith (πίστις, pistis) - Strong's G4102

2. Salvation (σωτηρία, soteria) - Strong's G4991

3. Believe (πιστεύω, pisteuo) - Strong's G4100

4. Grace (χάρις, charis) - Strong's G5485

5. Gift (δωρεά, dorea) - Strong's G1431

Expository Bible Study and Commentary

Ephesians 2:8-9 – Salvation as a Gift Through Faith

"For by grace (charis - G5485) you have been saved (sozo - G4982) through faith (pistis - G4102), and that not of yourselves; it is the gift (dorea - G1431) of God, not of works, lest anyone should boast."

- Strong's Analysis: "Grace" (charis - G5485) signifies unmerited favor, while "saved" (sozo - G4982) refers to deliverance from sin's penalty. "Gift" (dorea - G1431) emphasizes that salvation is freely given, unattainable through human effort.

- Commentary: This foundational verse underscores that salvation is entirely a work of God's grace, received by faith, not earned by human merit. Paul explicitly states that no one can boast of their salvation because it is God's gift, not a reward for works. The emphasis on grace points to the undeserved nature of salvation, making it clear that faith is the channel by which grace reaches individuals, yet even this faith is part of God's gift. Salvation, therefore, relies solely on God's initiative and not human effort.

Romans 10:9-10 – Confession and Belief in Salvation

"If you declare with your mouth, 'Jesus is Lord,' and believe (pisteuo - G4100) in your heart that God raised him from the dead, you will be saved (sozo - G4982). For it is with your heart that you believe and are justified, and it is with your mouth that you profess your faith and are saved."

- Strong's Analysis: "Believe" (pisteuo - G4100) means to place confidence in, while "saved" (sozo - G4982) emphasizes being delivered from sin's consequences.

- Commentary: Paul illustrates that salvation involves both inner belief and outward confession. Believing "in your heart" implies a genuine, wholehearted trust in Christ's resurrection and lordship. This belief is not merely intellectual but rooted in the core of one's being, resulting in a confession that Jesus is Lord. Salvation, therefore, is deeply personal and transformative, connecting belief with a life-changing faith that results in justification and public confession.

John 3:16 – Faith in the Promised Savior

"For God so loved the world that He gave His only begotten Son, that whoever believes (pisteuo - G4100) in Him should not perish but have everlasting life."

- Strong's Analysis: "Believes" (pisteuo - G4100) indicates an abiding trust in Jesus for eternal life, rooted in God's love and promise.

- Commentary: John emphasizes the accessibility of salvation through faith in Jesus. God's love is expressed through the sacrificial giving of His Son, with salvation offered to all who believe. This passage clarifies that faith in Jesus is the sole requirement for eternal life, underscoring salvation as a gracious gift. Faith here signifies reliance on Christ, transcending intellectual assent by embracing Jesus' role as Savior and entrusting one's eternal future to Him.

Titus 3:5-7 – Salvation by Mercy, Not by Works

"Not by works of righteousness which we have done, but according to His mercy He saved (sozo - G4982) us, through the washing of regeneration and renewing of the Holy Spirit, whom He poured out on us abundantly through Jesus Christ our Savior, that having been justified by His grace (charis - G5485), we should become heirs according to the hope of eternal life."

- Strong's Analysis: "Mercy" (eleos - G1656) signifies compassion in action, while "regeneration" (paliggenesia - G3824) suggests a new birth, and "grace" (charis - G5485) highlights undeserved kindness.

- Commentary: Paul contrasts human works with God's merciful act of salvation, which comes through the Holy Spirit's regenerating power. Salvation does not depend on any righteous deeds but solely on God's mercy, resulting in a new birth and renewal through the Spirit. This transformation, made possible by grace, marks believers as heirs of eternal life. Titus clarifies that salvation is comprehensive, encompassing justification, regeneration, and the hope of eternal life—all flowing from God's grace.

Hebrews 11:1, 6 – Faith as the Substance and Means of Pleasing God

"Now faith (pistis - G4102) is the substance of things hoped for, the evidence of things not seen... But without faith it is impossible to please Him, for he who comes to God must believe (pisteuo - G4100) that He is, and that He is a rewarder of those who diligently seek Him."

- Strong's Analysis: "Faith" (pistis - G4102) is described as both substance (confidence) and evidence, implying a firm foundation.

- Commentary: Hebrews defines faith as both assurance and conviction, central to a relationship with God. Pleasing God requires faith, which entails both belief in His existence and trust in His nature as a rewarder of those who earnestly seek Him. This verse teaches that faith is foundational, not just for salvation but for a life that aligns with God's will. Without faith, no meaningful connection with God can be established, as faith is the key to pleasing Him.

Theological Insights on Faith and Salvation

1. Salvation as a Divine Gift: Ephesians 2:8-9 and Titus 3:5-7 emphasize that salvation is a free gift, stemming from God's mercy and grace rather than human achievement. The concept of grace highlights God's initiative in salvation, making it clear that human works cannot contribute to one's justification. Salvation as a gift points to the undeserved

nature of grace, with faith being the channel through which this grace is received.

2. Faith as Transformative Belief: Romans 10:9-10 and John 3:16 illustrate that faith in Christ is not simply intellectual acknowledgment but a transformative belief that shapes one's heart and actions. Faith is more than mental assent; it involves a trust in God that motivates both inward transformation and outward confession, ultimately affecting every aspect of the believer's life.

3. The Role of Faith in Pleasing God: Hebrews 11:1, 6 underscores that faith is essential for pleasing God, as it involves both belief in His existence and confidence in His promises. Faith allows believers to align with God's will and purposes, establishing a dynamic relationship with Him. It is by faith that believers trust in God's promises, even when they are unseen, making faith essential for a life that honors God.

Practical Applications of Faith in Salvation

- Embracing Grace Through Faith: Recognizing that salvation is God's gift prevents believers from relying on personal achievements and directs them to trust fully in Christ's redemptive work. This grace-based faith encourages humility, gratitude, and confidence in God's promise of eternal life.

- Confession and Action as Expressions of Faith: As Romans 10:9-10 suggests, genuine faith leads to confession and a life that reflects belief in Jesus' lordship. Believers are encouraged to express their faith in both words and actions, affirming their commitment to live in a way that honors God's gift of salvation.

- Living with Assurance and Hope: Understanding faith as the "substance of things hoped for" (Hebrews 11:1) gives believers assurance in God's promises. Faith empowers believers to live with hope, knowing that salvation is secure and that God will fulfill His promises. This assurance impacts daily life, fostering a deep trust in God's character and faithfulness.

This study of faith and salvation as a divine gift helps to clarify the depth and breadth of God's work in the believer's life. It underscores that while belief is foundational, true faith goes further, resulting in a trust that transforms and leads to salvation as God's precious, unearned gift.

CHAPTER 11

NURTURING FAITH BEYOND BELIEF

Once faith moves beyond belief and is embraced as a life-transforming trust in God, it becomes essential to nurture that faith. Like any relationship, our faith must be cultivated, deepened, and maintained through intentional practices and disciplines. Faith is not static; it can grow stronger over time or become weakened if neglected. In this chapter, we will explore practical ways to nurture and strengthen faith, drawing from theological insights, prayer practices, biblical meditation, and spiritual disciplines that cultivate a deeper, enduring trust in God.

The Importance of Nurturing Faith

Faith is described in Scripture as a dynamic and growing reality in the life of a believer. 2 Peter 3:18 encourages us to:

"Grow in the grace and knowledge of our Lord and Savior Jesus Christ."

This growth implies that faith must be nurtured, like a seed that, once planted, requires care and attention to flourish.

Faith, while initially a gift from God, also requires cooperation from us. Just as we nourish our physical bodies with food, water, and rest, we must nourish our spiritual lives with practices that deepen our relationship with God. Faith is not simply a one-time event but a lifelong journey that demands continuous attention and effort. As faith grows, it becomes more steadfast, able to withstand trials, temptations, and the complexities of life.

The Apostle Paul speaks of this nurturing process in Colossians 2:6-7:

"So then, just as you received Christ Jesus as Lord, continue to live your lives in Him, rooted and built up in Him, strengthened in the faith as you were taught, and overflowing with thankfulness."

This passage reminds us that, after receiving Christ, we must continue to live in Him, actively building up our faith and becoming rooted in God's truth.

Spiritual Disciplines That Nurture Faith

Nurturing faith requires intentional spiritual disciplines. These practices, when regularly observed, deepen our relationship with God, build spiritual strength, and transform belief into enduring faith. Below are several key disciplines that help nurture faith.

1. Prayer: Communion with God

Prayer is the lifeline of faith. Through prayer, we communicate with God, express our trust in Him, and open ourselves to His guidance. It is in the practice of prayer that we nurture our relationship with God, grow in our dependence on Him, and experience His presence in our lives.

Philippians 4:6-7 encourages us to approach God with everything through prayer:

"Do not be anxious about anything, but in every situation, by prayer and petition, with thanksgiving, present your requests to God. And the peace of God, which transcends all understanding, will guard your hearts and your minds in Christ Jesus."

When we make prayer a regular part of our lives, we nurture our faith by continually bringing our needs, hopes, and fears to God, trusting Him to act according to His will. Prayer reminds us of God's sovereignty and goodness, helping us to place our trust in Him, especially in times of uncertainty.

Practical ways to deepen your prayer life include setting aside regular times for prayer, incorporating prayers of gratitude, and praying the Scriptures. Praying in community with other believers can also strengthen personal faith and create a powerful shared experience of God's presence.

2. Meditation on Scripture: Feeding the Mind and Spirit

Biblical meditation is a practice of dwelling on God's Word, allowing it to penetrate deeply into our hearts and minds. Scripture is foundational to nurturing faith, as it reveals God's character, promises, and will for our lives.

Romans 10:17 reminds us that:

"Faith comes from hearing, and hearing by the word of Christ."

When we meditate on the Bible, we give the Holy Spirit the opportunity to transform our thinking and help us see our lives and the world through the lens of God's truth. Meditation on Scripture moves beyond reading for information to engaging with the text in a way that applies it personally and intimately to our daily lives.

Practical ways to meditate on Scripture include memorizing key verses, practicing Lectio Divina (a contemplative way of reading the Bible), and journaling about insights gained through Bible study. Focusing on God's promises during times of uncertainty or trial can help strengthen faith by reminding us of His unchanging character.

3. Worship: Expressing Faith in God's Worthiness

Worship is both an act of faith and a means of nurturing faith. When we worship, we declare the greatness of God, align our hearts with His will, and express our trust in His power and goodness.

Psalm 95:6-7 calls us into worship:

"Come, let us bow down in worship, let us kneel before the Lord our Maker; for He is our God and we are the people of His pasture, the flock under His care."

Worship, whether through singing, prayer, or silent adoration, allows us to shift our focus from ourselves to God. It strengthens faith by reminding us of God's majesty and sovereignty and reinforces the truth that He is in control of our lives. Worship nurtures faith by grounding it in the reality of who God is and the promises He has made.

Engaging in both personal and corporate worship is essential for a vibrant faith. Singing hymns or worship songs, participating in the sacraments, and attending church services are practical ways to incorporate worship into your spiritual life.

4. Fasting: Focusing on God

Fasting is a discipline that involves voluntarily giving up something, often food, for a period of time to focus more intently on God. Fasting is a way to humble ourselves, express our dependence on God, and draw closer to Him. It nurtures faith by stripping away distractions and reminding us that our ultimate satisfaction comes from God alone.

Jesus assumes that His followers will fast, as seen in Matthew 6:16-18, where He says:

"When you fast, do not look somber as the hypocrites do, for they disfigure their faces to show others they are fasting. Truly I tell you, they have received their reward in full."

Fasting, when combined with prayer and meditation on Scripture, is a powerful way to deepen trust in God. It creates space for spiritual growth and helps refocus our hearts on what truly matters. Fasting can be practiced in a variety of ways, including giving up food, social media, or other activities for a designated time in order to focus more on God.

5. Fellowship: Nurturing Faith in Community

Faith is not meant to be lived out in isolation. Christian community provides essential support, encouragement, and accountability. Hebrews 10:24-25 emphasizes the importance of fellowship:

"And let us consider how we may spur one another on toward love and good deeds, not giving up meeting together, as some are in the habit of doing, but encouraging one another—and all the more as you see the Day approaching."

Fellowship with other believers nurtures faith by creating an environment where we can learn from one another, share our struggles, and celebrate our victories in Christ. In times of doubt or difficulty, the encouragement of fellow believers helps us remain grounded in our faith and reminds us of God's faithfulness.

Practical ways to nurture faith through fellowship include joining a small group or Bible study, serving in ministry alongside other believers, and building strong Christian friendships where mutual encouragement and accountability can flourish.

Trusting God Through Trials: Strengthening Faith in Difficult Times

One of the greatest challenges to faith comes in times of trial. Difficulties, suffering, and unanswered prayers can shake our trust in God. However, Scripture teaches that trials are opportunities to strengthen and refine our faith.

James 1:2-4 encourages believers to embrace trials as part of the faith journey:

"Consider it pure joy, my brothers and sisters, whenever you face trials of many kinds, because you know that the testing of your faith produces perseverance. Let perseverance finish its work so that you may be mature and complete, not lacking anything."

Trials test the genuineness of our faith, but they also provide opportunities for growth. When we endure hardship with a heart of trust and submission to God, our faith becomes more resilient. During these times, nurturing faith through prayer, Scripture, and fellowship becomes even more crucial.

One of the keys to trusting God in trials is remembering His faithfulness in the past. Reflecting on the ways God has answered prayers, provided in times of need, and fulfilled His promises in Scripture can strengthen our faith and help us persevere through difficult seasons.

Faith That Perseveres: Long-Term Commitment to God's Will

Finally, nurturing faith involves a long-term commitment to God's will. Faith is not just for moments of inspiration or spiritual highs; it is a day-to-day commitment to walk with God through all of life's ups and downs. Hebrews 12:1-2 encourages believers to persevere in faith:

"Therefore, since we are surrounded by such a great cloud of witnesses, let us throw off everything that hinders and the sin that so easily entangles. And let us run with perseverance the race marked out for us, fixing our eyes on Jesus, the pioneer and perfecter of faith."

Faith that endures is faith that continually looks to Jesus as the ultimate example and source of strength. He is the author and perfecter of our faith, and by keeping our eyes fixed on Him, we can run the race with perseverance.

Cultivating an Enduring Faith

Nurturing faith beyond belief is essential for every Christian. It is a lifelong process of deepening trust in God, growing in spiritual maturity, and living in alignment with God's will. Through prayer, meditation on Scripture, worship, fasting, and fellowship, we cultivate a faith that is strong, steadfast, and capable of withstanding the trials of life.

As we continue to nurture our faith, we are transformed into the image of Christ, becoming more like Him in character, thought, and action. Faith is not just something we believe—it is something we live. And as we nurture that faith, it becomes an enduring source of strength, hope, and joy, allowing us to experience the fullness of life in Christ.

Supplements to Chapter 11: "Nurturing Faith Beyond Belief" Expository Bible Study and Commentary with Strong's Concordance

In this chapter, we focus on the practical aspects of deepening faith beyond initial belief, encouraging believers to cultivate a relationship with God through spiritual disciplines, commitment, and perseverance. Moving beyond belief means maturing in trust, reliance, and obedience, thus nurturing a faith that impacts all areas of life. This chapter emphasizes how regular spiritual practices help believers maintain and deepen their faith, fostering a profound connection with God that transforms their daily lives.

Key Terms in Strong's Concordance

1. Faith (πίστις, pistis) - Strong's G4102
2. Believe (πιστεύω, pisteuo) - Strong's G4100
3. Obedience (ὑπακοή, hupakoe) - Strong's G5218
4. Abide (μένω, meno) - Strong's G3306
5. Endurance (ὑπομονή, hupomone) - Strong's G5281
6. Meditate (μελετάω, meletao) - Strong's G3191

Expository Bible Study and Commentary

James 1:2-4 – Nurturing Faith Through Trials

"Consider it pure joy, my brothers and sisters, whenever you face trials of many kinds, because you know that the testing of your faith (pistis - G4102) produces perseverance (hupomone - G5281). Let perseverance finish its work so that you may be mature and complete, not lacking anything."

- Strong's Analysis: "Faith" (pistis - G4102) here refers to a steadfast trust, while "perseverance" (hupomone - G5281) means endurance or patient waiting.

- Commentary: James encourages believers to view trials as opportunities to grow in faith. When faith is "tested," endurance develops, leading to spiritual maturity and completeness. This passage emphasizes the role of difficulties in nurturing a resilient faith that relies on God. Growth in faith often comes through challenges that encourage deeper dependence on God's promises, refining the believer's trust and commitment.

John 15:4-5 – Abiding in Christ for Spiritual Growth

"Abide (meno - G3306) in Me, and I in you. As the branch cannot bear fruit of itself, unless it abides in the vine, neither can you, unless you abide in Me. I am the vine, you are the branches. He who abides in Me, and I in him, bears much fruit; for without Me you can do nothing."

- Strong's Analysis: "Abide" (meno - G3306) means to remain, stay, or dwell, indicating a consistent, intimate connection.

- Commentary: Jesus calls His followers to "abide" in Him, illustrating that spiritual fruitfulness and growth come from a sustained, ongoing relationship with Him. This abiding is central to nurturing faith beyond belief, as it involves daily dependence on Christ as the source of spiritual life. Abiding nurtures a heart that grows in love, trust, and obedience, with faith strengthened through close communion with God.

Romans 10:17 – The Role of Scripture in Building Faith

"So then faith (pistis - G4102) comes by hearing, and hearing by the word of God."

- Strong's Analysis: "Faith" (pistis - G4102) here relates to conviction and reliance on the truth of God's Word.

- Commentary: Paul underscores the importance of Scripture in nurturing faith. Regularly engaging with God's Word helps build trust in His promises and deepen understanding of His nature. Through reading, meditating on, and internalizing the Bible, believers strengthen their faith, allowing it to go beyond intellectual belief and becoming an active, lived-out trust in God's faithfulness.

Colossians 3:16 – Faith Nurtured by Worship and Community

"Let the word of Christ dwell (enoikeo - G1774) in you richly in all wisdom, teaching and admonishing one another in psalms and hymns and spiritual songs, singing with grace in your hearts to the Lord."

- Strong's Analysis: "Dwell" (enoikeo - G1774) means to inhabit or take residence, implying the Word's transforming influence within.

- Commentary: Paul encourages believers to allow the Word of Christ to dwell richly within them, emphasizing worship and communal encouragement. Singing, teaching, and learning within a faith community all serve to nurture faith, transforming belief into active, shared faith. This communal aspect of spiritual growth reminds believers that faith is cultivated not only in solitude but also through encouragement, guidance, and accountability within the body of Christ.

Hebrews 12:1-2 – Fixing Our Eyes on Jesus as a Source of Endurance

"Let us run with endurance (hupomone - G5281) the race that is set before us, looking unto Jesus, the author and finisher of our faith (pistis - G4102), who for the joy that was set before Him endured the cross, despising the shame, and has sat down at the right hand of the throne of God."

- Strong's Analysis: "Endurance" (hupomone - G5281) here speaks to steadfast patience, while "faith" (pistis - G4102) signifies a trusting reliance on Jesus.

- Commentary: Hebrews encourages believers to look to Jesus as both the initiator and perfecter of faith. By focusing on His example and drawing strength from His endurance, believers are equipped to persevere in their own faith journey. This passage teaches that nurturing faith involves an intentional focus on Jesus, allowing His life and sacrifice to inspire trust, patience, and commitment to God's purposes.

Practical Steps for Nurturing Faith Beyond Belief

1. Engage with Scripture Regularly: Romans 10:17 emphasizes that faith is built by hearing the Word of God. By studying, memorizing, and meditating on Scripture, believers deepen their understanding of God's promises, fueling their trust in Him.

2. Prioritize Prayer and Meditation: Philippians 4:6-7 encourages believers to bring their requests to God in prayer, which not only strengthens faith but brings peace. Meditation on God's Word (Psalm 1:2) allows His truth to permeate the mind and heart, fostering a faith that goes beyond simple belief.

3. Embrace Community and Worship: Colossians 3:16 shows how worship and fellowship with other believers nurture faith. Engaging with the church community provides accountability, encouragement, and wisdom, helping believers grow in faith through shared experiences and teachings.

4. Seek to Persevere Through Trials: James 1:2-4 and Hebrews 12:1-2 emphasize perseverance. Facing trials with patience and a reliance on God's strength nurtures a resilient faith. Reflecting on Jesus' endurance and His purpose for

believers can provide motivation to persevere and grow in trust.

5. Practice Obedience and Application: Living out faith through obedience (James 1:22) reinforces trust in God's guidance. Applying biblical principles in daily life allows faith to mature beyond intellectual belief, becoming a defining characteristic of the believer's life.

Theological Insights on Nurturing Faith

- The Role of the Holy Spirit: Ephesians 3:16-17 speaks of believers being strengthened in faith through the Spirit's power. This strengthening comes as believers surrender to the Spirit's work, cultivating a faith rooted in love and understanding of Christ.

- Abiding as Sustaining Faith: John 15:4-5 illustrates that abiding in Christ is central to spiritual growth. The act of continually dwelling in Him reinforces a relationship based on trust, dependence, and love, which moves faith beyond mere intellectual belief.

- Faith as a Communal Journey: Colossians 3:16 and Hebrews 10:24-25 highlight that faith flourishes in a community. The encouragement and guidance found within a church setting provide support, accountability, and a shared commitment to Christ's teachings.

Nurturing faith beyond belief involves intentional steps of trust, commitment, and reliance on God. Through regular engagement with Scripture, prayer, fellowship, and perseverance, faith grows from mere belief into a steadfast relationship with God. This faith is characterized by resilience in trials, joy in worship, and active obedience. As believers nurture their faith, they experience a transformation that reaches into every aspect of their lives, fulfilling the call to live by faith and not by sight.

CHAPTER 12

LIVING FAITH BEYOND BELIEF

Throughout this book, we have explored the theological and practical distinctions between faith and belief. Belief, while foundational to the Christian life, is only the beginning of a relationship with God. It is the intellectual acknowledgment of truth, the recognition of God's existence, and the acceptance of the gospel message. However, it is faith that takes belief deeper, transforming it into a living, dynamic relationship with God.

In this concluding chapter, we will summarize how faith sustains and nurtures the life of a believer, moving beyond mere intellectual assent to embrace a life marked by trust, obedience, and action. The distinction between faith and belief is not just theological—it is practical and impacts every aspect of our relationship with God and how we live our daily lives.

Belief: The Entry Point

Belief is the necessary entry point to the Christian life. It is the initial response to the gospel message, the moment when we recognize the truth of who Jesus is and what He has done for us. John 3:16 encapsulates the importance of belief:

"For God so loved the world that He gave His one and only Son, that whoever believes in Him shall not perish but have eternal life."

Belief in Jesus Christ as Savior is the key to receiving eternal life. It opens the door to a relationship with God and is the foundation upon which everything else in the Christian life is built. But belief alone, as we have seen, is not enough. It must be nurtured and transformed into faith, which goes beyond accepting facts to trusting in God personally and completely.

Faith: The Sustaining Force

While belief is the entry point, faith is what sustains our relationship with God. Faith turns belief into action, trust, and obedience. It is faith that compels us to follow God's will, even when we cannot see the full picture or understand His plans. Faith allows us to live in the assurance of God's promises, trusting Him in both the good times and the difficult ones.

Hebrews 11:1 defines faith as:

"Now faith is confidence in what we hope for and assurance about what we do not see."

Faith goes beyond intellectual belief and becomes a deep trust in the unseen, a reliance on God's character and promises. It is what moves us to act in obedience, even when the road ahead is uncertain. As we have seen through the examples of Abraham, Noah, and others in the "Hall of Faith," true faith is not passive—it is active, alive, and transformative. Faith is the driving force behind our relationship with God, propelling us forward in trust, obedience, and action.

Faith Transforms Our Relationship with God

One of the key distinctions between faith and belief is the way faith transforms our relationship with God. Belief acknowledges God's existence and the truth of His word, but faith turns that belief into a personal, living relationship. Faith is what allows us to experience God not just as an abstract being but as a personal Savior, Lord, and friend.

Faith deepens our intimacy with God, inviting us to rely on Him, trust in His goodness, and follow His lead in every area of our lives. This relationship of trust is central to living a life of faith. Proverbs 3:5-6 encourages us:

"Trust in the Lord with all your heart and lean not on your own understanding; in all your ways submit to Him, and He will make your paths straight."

Living by faith means submitting to God's will, even when it conflicts with our understanding or desires. It is the act of placing our full confidence in God, trusting that He knows what is best for us and that His plans are good. This deep, abiding trust transforms the way we live, making faith the foundation of every decision and action we take.

Obedience: Faith in Action

Faith is not just about internal trust; it is about external obedience. True faith leads to action, compelling us to live out the commands of God in our daily lives. James 2:26 reminds us that:

"As the body without the spirit is dead, so faith without deeds is dead."

Living in faith means putting our trust in God into practice. It means loving our neighbors, serving others, and living a life that reflects the values and principles of the gospel. Faith calls us to step out in obedience, even when it is difficult, inconvenient, or risky. It is through obedience that our faith is made complete, as we align our actions with our trust in God.

Jesus Himself emphasized the connection between faith and obedience in John 14:15, saying:

"If you love me, keep my commands."

Obedience is the natural outflow of faith. When we trust in God, we naturally desire to live according to His will. Our faith compels us to follow Him, not out of obligation but out of love and trust in His goodness.

The Growth of Faith: A Lifelong Journey

Faith is not a one-time event but a lifelong journey. As we walk with God, our faith deepens and grows. Trials, challenges, and even doubts can become opportunities for our faith to be strengthened. James 1:2-4 speaks to this process of growth:

"Consider it pure joy, my brothers and sisters, whenever you face trials of many kinds, because you know that the testing of your faith produces perseverance. Let perseverance finish its work so that you may be mature and complete, not lacking anything."

Faith grows as we trust God in difficult circumstances, relying on His strength rather than our own. Over time, as we see God's faithfulness in our lives, our trust in Him deepens. What began as belief matures into a faith that is steadfast, enduring, and able to withstand the challenges of life.

Nurturing faith through prayer, Scripture, worship, and community (as explored in Chapter 11) is essential for this growth. These spiritual disciplines help us to keep our focus on God and to trust Him more fully as we walk through the joys and trials of life.

Faith and God's Purpose for Our Lives

Faith also shapes how we understand and live out God's purpose for our lives. When we live in faith, we trust that God has a plan for us, even if we do not fully understand it. Jeremiah 29:11 reassures us of this truth:

"For I know the plans I have for you," declares the Lord, "plans to prosper you and not to harm you, plans to give you hope and a future."

Faith allows us to surrender our own desires and ambitions to God, trusting that His plans are greater than our own. As we live in faith, we align our lives with His purpose, finding meaning, direction, and fulfillment in following His will. This trust in God's purpose gives us the confidence to live boldly, stepping into the unknown with the assurance that God is with us.

Moving Beyond Belief: A Life of Faith

In conclusion, the distinction between faith and belief is not just theological—it is profoundly practical. Belief is the entry point to a relationship with God, but faith is what sustains that relationship and transforms it into a vibrant, living connection. Faith moves us beyond mere intellectual acknowledgment into a life characterized by trust, obedience, and action.

As we grow in faith, we experience the fullness of life in Christ. We move beyond simply believing in God's existence to trusting Him with every aspect of our lives. Our faith compels us to follow God's will, to serve others, and to live with the confidence that God's promises are true and His purposes for us are good.

Faith is the key to living a life that honors God and fulfills His calling for us. It is not just something we believe—it is something we live, day by day, moment by moment, in trust and obedience to the One who is faithful and true. And as we continue to live in faith, we discover the depth of God's love, the joy of His presence, and the peace that comes from walking with Him.

Supplements to Chapter 12: "Living Faith Beyond Belief" Expository Bible Study and Commentary with Strong's Concordance

This final chapter explores what it means to move from intellectual belief to a living, active faith that permeates all aspects of life. Living faith goes beyond acknowledging doctrinal truths; it involves a transformative relationship with God, marked by trust, obedience, and an ongoing commitment to His will. This study examines how living faith is exemplified in Scripture, emphasizing how believers can practically live out their faith through sustained spiritual disciplines and actions.

Key Terms in Strong's Concordance

1. Faith (πίστις, pistis) - Strong's G4102

2. Believe (πιστεύω, pisteuo) - Strong's G4100

3. Works (ἔργα, erga) - Strong's G2041

4. Walk (περιπατέω, peripateo) - Strong's G4043

5. Life (ζωή, zoe) - Strong's G2222

6. Hope (ἐλπίς, elpis) - Strong's G1680

Expository Bible Study and Commentary

Galatians 2:20 – Faith as a New Life in Christ

"I have been crucified with Christ; it is no longer I who live, but Christ lives in me; and the life (zoe - G2222) which I now live in the flesh I live by faith (pistis - G4102) in the Son of God, who loved me and gave Himself for me."

- Strong's Analysis: "Life" (zoe - G2222) refers to a spiritual, God-given life, distinct from mere physical existence, while "faith" (pistis - G4102) emphasizes trusting, relational belief.

- Commentary: Paul's declaration underscores that living faith means allowing Christ to live through us. His faith wasn't just intellectual or emotional; it represented a complete transformation in identity and purpose. For believers, living faith entails surrendering personal desires and allowing Christ's love and purpose to shape every decision. This verse emphasizes that faith transforms the believer's entire being, leading to a life that reflects Christ's presence and values.

James 2:17 – Faith and Works Together

"Thus also faith (pistis - G4102) by itself, if it does not have works (erga - G2041), is dead."

- Strong's Analysis: "Faith" (pistis - G4102) here indicates active trust and belief, while "works" (erga - G2041) refers to deeds or actions that embody that trust.

- Commentary: James highlights that faith without corresponding actions is "dead," lacking vitality. Living faith manifests in visible actions, demonstrating that faith is real and impactful. When believers live out their faith, it's reflected in choices, behaviors, and relationships, providing evidence of their inner transformation. James's teaching reminds us that while faith begins with belief, it matures into a life marked by compassionate, Christ-centered actions.

2 Corinthians 5:7 – Walking by Faith, Not by Sight

"For we walk (peripateo - G4043) by faith (pistis - G4102), not by sight."

- Strong's Analysis: "Walk" (peripateo - G4043) implies ongoing, habitual movement, while "faith" (pistis - G4102) denotes confident reliance on God.

- Commentary: Paul contrasts the natural tendency to rely on what is seen with the spiritual discipline of trusting God beyond visible circumstances. Walking by faith signifies an ongoing choice to trust God's wisdom and promises, even when outcomes are unclear. Living faith, then, is expressed by continually choosing trust over fear, grounded in the assurance that God is in control. This approach requires maturity, as believers learn to lean on spiritual truths rather than temporary, visible conditions.

Hebrews 10:22-23 – Holding Fast to Hope

"Let us draw near with a true heart in full assurance of faith (pistis - G4102), having our hearts sprinkled from an evil conscience and our bodies washed with pure water. Let us hold fast the confession of our hope (elpis - G1680) without wavering, for He who promised is faithful."

- Strong's Analysis: "Faith" (pistis - G4102) is the foundation of assurance, while "hope" (elpis - G1680) represents the confident expectation based on God's promises.

- Commentary: Living faith holds steadfastly to hope, grounded in God's faithfulness. The writer of Hebrews encourages believers to remain committed to their faith, drawing near to God with a cleansed conscience and pure devotion. Living faith doesn't waver but grows stronger through hope, trusting that God's promises are unbreakable. In practical terms, living out faith requires believers to seek God wholeheartedly, confident in His trustworthiness.

Romans 12:1-2 – Faith as a Daily Act of Worship

"I beseech you therefore, brethren, by the mercies of God, that you present your bodies a living sacrifice, holy, acceptable to God, which is your reasonable service. And do not be conformed to this world, but be transformed by the renewing of your mind, that you may prove what is that good and acceptable and perfect will of God."

- Strong's Analysis: Although "faith" isn't explicitly mentioned here, the concept of "reasonable service" or worship embodies living faith through action and devotion.

- Commentary: Paul exhorts believers to live out their faith by offering themselves fully to God as an act of spiritual worship. A life of faith doesn't merely involve church attendance or intellectual belief; it requires total devotion to God's will, rejecting worldly influences, and aligning one's actions with God's values. Living faith, then, transforms both heart and mind, influencing every aspect of the believer's life as they seek to honor God in daily choices.

Practical Applications for Living Faith

1. Daily Dependence on God: Galatians 2:20 emphasizes that living faith means allowing Christ's life to work through us. This calls for a daily surrender, relying on God for strength, wisdom, and guidance in every area of life.

2. Consistency in Good Works: James 2:17 shows that living faith requires corresponding actions. Believers can practice this by seeking opportunities to serve others, being generous, and showing kindness, which embody Christ's love.

3. Choosing Faith Over Fear: Walking by faith, as encouraged in 2 Corinthians 5:7, involves making intentional choices to trust God, especially in difficult circumstances. Believers can remind themselves of God's promises, resisting the urge to rely solely on what is visible.

4. Holding Onto Hope: Hebrews 10:22-23 calls for a confident hope. Practically, this means grounding one's outlook in God's faithfulness, allowing hope to shape decisions and attitudes instead of being swayed by temporary challenges.

5. Transformative Worship: Romans 12:1-2 suggests that living faith is a daily act of worship. Believers nurture living faith by prioritizing time with God, renewing their minds through Scripture, and seeking to live in alignment with His will in every aspect of life.

Theological Insights on Living Faith

- Faith as the Foundation of Spiritual Growth: A living faith doesn't stagnate; it grows through continual reliance on God's Word, fellowship, and the Spirit's guidance.

- The Role of the Holy Spirit: Living faith relies on the Holy Spirit, who provides strength and insight as believers navigate their journey with God (Galatians 5:16).

- Integration of Faith and Works: The balance between faith and works (James 2:17) underscores that while faith is foundational, it must produce tangible actions to be alive and meaningful.

Living faith moves beyond intellectual belief, manifesting as a transformative, daily relationship with God. Believers are called to live out their faith with devotion, consistency, and perseverance, anchoring themselves in God's promises. Faith becomes a lens through which every action, decision, and relationship is viewed, resulting in a life that honors God and demonstrates His love to others. This active, enduring faith is what pleases God, fulfilling the call to live not just as believers, but as disciples committed to embodying the heart and mission of Christ in the world.

CHAPTER 13

VERSES ON FAITH AND BELIEF

A comprehensive list of Bible verses on faith and belief, touching on various aspects, such as the nature, importance, and practical applications of faith and belief:

Verses on Faith

1. Hebrews 11:1 - "Now faith is the substance of things hoped for, the evidence of things not seen."

2. Ephesians 2:8-9 - "For by grace you have been saved through faith, and that not of yourselves; it is the gift of God, not of works, lest anyone should boast."

3. Romans 10:17 - "So then faith comes by hearing, and hearing by the word of God."

4. 2 Corinthians 5:7 - "For we walk by faith, not by sight."

5. James 2:17 - "Thus also faith by itself, if it does not have works, is dead."

6. Hebrews 11:6 - "But without faith it is impossible to please Him, for he who comes to God must believe that He is, and that He is a rewarder of those who diligently seek Him."

7. Mark 11:22-24 - "So Jesus answered and said to them, 'Have faith in God. For assuredly, I say to you, whoever says to this mountain, 'Be removed and be cast into the sea,' and does not doubt in his heart, but believes that those things he says will be done, he will have whatever he says. Therefore I say to you, whatever things you ask when you pray, believe that you receive them, and you will have them.'"

8. Galatians 2:20 - "I have been crucified with Christ; it is no longer I who live, but Christ lives in me; and the life which I now live in the flesh I live by faith in the Son of God, who loved me and gave Himself for me."

9. 1 Peter 1:8-9 - "Whom having not seen, you love. Though now you do not see Him, yet believing, you rejoice

with joy inexpressible and full of glory, receiving the end of your faith—the salvation of your souls."

10. James 1:3 - "Knowing that the testing of your faith produces patience."

11. Romans 1:17 - "For in it the righteousness of God is revealed from faith to faith; as it is written, 'The just shall live by faith.'"

12. 1 Corinthians 16:13 - "Watch, stand fast in the faith, be brave, be strong."

13. 1 John 5:4 - "For whatever is born of God overcomes the world. And this is the victory that has overcome the world—our faith."

14. Matthew 21:22 - "And whatever things you ask in prayer, believing, you will receive."

15. Luke 17:6 - "So the Lord said, 'If you have faith as a mustard seed, you can say to this mulberry tree, 'Be pulled up by the roots and be planted in the sea,' and it would obey you.'"

16. Romans 12:3 - "For I say, through the grace given to me, to everyone who is among you, not to think of himself more highly than he ought to think, but to think soberly, as God has dealt to each one a measure of faith."

17. Galatians 3:26 - "For you are all sons of God through faith in Christ Jesus."

18. Philippians 3:9 - "And be found in Him, not having my own righteousness, which is from the law, but that which is through faith in Christ, the righteousness which is from God by faith."

Verses on Belief and Believing

1. John 3:16 - "For God so loved the world that He gave His only begotten Son, that whoever believes in Him should not perish but have everlasting life."

2. Mark 9:23 - "Jesus said to him, 'If you can believe, all things are possible to him who believes.'"

3. John 6:29 - "Jesus answered and said to them, 'This is the work of God, that you believe in Him whom He sent.'"

4. John 11:25-26 - "Jesus said to her, 'I am the resurrection and the life. He who believes in Me, though he may die, he shall live. And whoever lives and believes in Me shall never die. Do you believe this?'"

5. John 1:12 - "But as many as received Him, to them He gave the right to become children of God, to those who believe in His name."

6. Romans 10:9-10 - "That if you confess with your mouth the Lord Jesus and believe in your heart that God has raised Him from the dead, you will be saved. For with the heart one believes unto righteousness, and with the mouth confession is made unto salvation."

7. John 20:29 - "Jesus said to him, 'Thomas, because you have seen Me, you have believed. Blessed are those who have not seen and yet have believed.'"

8. Acts 16:31 - "So they said, 'Believe on the Lord Jesus Christ, and you will be saved, you and your household.'"

9. 1 John 5:10 - "He who believes in the Son of God has the witness in himself; he who does not believe God has

made Him a liar, because he has not believed the testimony that God has given of His Son."

10. James 2:19 - "You believe that there is one God. You do well. Even the demons believe—and tremble!"

11. Mark 5:36 - "As soon as Jesus heard the word that was spoken, He said to the ruler of the synagogue, 'Do not be afraid; only believe.'"

12. John 14:1 - "Let not your heart be troubled; you believe in God, believe also in Me."

13. John 8:24 - "Therefore I said to you that you will die in your sins; for if you do not believe that I am He, you will die in your sins."

14. Matthew 21:21-22 - "So Jesus answered and said to them, 'Assuredly, I say to you, if you have faith and do not doubt, you will not only do what was done to the fig tree, but also if you say to this mountain, 'Be removed and be cast into the sea,' it will be done. And whatever things you ask in prayer, believing, you will receive.'"

15. John 7:38 - "He who believes in Me, as the Scripture has said, out of his heart will flow rivers of living water."

16. 1 John 3:23 - "And this is His commandment: that we should believe on the name of His Son Jesus Christ and love one another, as He gave us commandment."

These passages underscore that belief is often the first step—a cognitive acknowledgment of God's truth—while faith incorporates belief but goes beyond it, encompassing trust, action, and a commitment to living out that belief. Together, they create a powerful dynamic for the Christian life.

CHAPTER 14

THEOLOGICAL QUESTIONS AND ANSWERS

Here's a set of questions and answers to deepen understanding of each chapter on the theological distinctions between faith and believing:

Chapter 1: Introduction to Faith and Believing

Q1: Why is understanding the difference between faith and belief important for Christians?

A1: Understanding this difference helps Christians build a deeper relationship with God, recognizing that belief is the intellectual acceptance of truth, while faith is an active, committed trust in God that involves the whole being.

Q2: How are faith and believing different in the Christian journey?

A2: Believing is accepting God's truth as real, whereas faith goes beyond acceptance, involving trust, action, and obedience, thereby defining a living, ongoing relationship with God.

Chapter 2: Defining Faith: The Heart of Christian Theology

Q1: What does the Greek word for faith, "pistis," imply?

A1: "Pistis" implies trust, fidelity, and loyalty, reflecting a deeper level of commitment beyond mere belief, involving a heartfelt reliance on God.

Q2: How does Hebrews 11:1 define faith, and what does this mean for Christians?

A2: Hebrews 11:1 defines faith as "the substance of things hoped for, the evidence of things not seen," meaning faith gives reality to hopes and confidence in unseen spiritual truths, guiding Christians to trust God's promises even when they're not visible.

Chapter 3: Believing: The Starting Point

Q1: What is the primary function of believing in Christianity?

A1: Believing serves as the entry point to the Christian faith, where one intellectually acknowledges the truth of God, Jesus Christ, and the gospel.

Q2: Why is believing alone insufficient without faith?

A2: Believing without faith does not lead to a transformed life. As James 2:19 points out, even demons believe in God's existence, but without trust and commitment, belief alone doesn't create a saving relationship with God.

Chapter 4: Faith as Trust and Commitment

Q1: How does faith differ from belief in its practical application?

A1: Faith is belief in action; it involves a commitment to trust in God's character and promises, leading to obedience and actions aligned with His will, even without full understanding.

Q2: What example from the Bible illustrates faith as trust and commitment?

A2: Abraham's story in Romans 4:3 shows faith as trust and commitment; he believed and acted upon God's promises, demonstrating unwavering trust even in the face of uncertainty.

Chapter 5: The Relationship Between Faith and Belief

Q1: How are faith and belief interconnected?

A1: Belief is foundational for faith; faith begins with belief in God's truth but deepens into trust, reliance, and a lifestyle of commitment to God's will.

Q2: How does the story of Thomas demonstrate the progression from belief to faith?

A2: In John 20:24-29, Thomas initially struggled to believe in Jesus' resurrection, but when he encountered Jesus, his belief transformed into faith—a deeper trust that declared Jesus as "Lord and God."

Chapter 6: Biblical Perspectives on Faith and Believing

Q1: How does James 2:14-26 highlight the difference between faith and belief?

A1: James emphasizes that faith without works is dead, showing that belief alone is insufficient without the evidence of faith through action.

Q2: What do the stories of the centurion and the woman with the issue of blood reveal about faith?

A2: Both stories show faith as action: the centurion (Matthew 8:5-13) and the woman (Mark 5:25-34) acted on their belief, showing trust in Jesus' ability to heal and save.

Chapter 7: The Role of Grace in Faith and Believing

Q1: According to Ephesians 2:8-9, what is the role of grace in faith?

A1: Grace is God's unmerited gift that enables faith; it is not from ourselves, but a gift that draws us into a saving relationship with Him, preventing any boasting in human effort.

Q2: How does grace make faith possible?

A2: Grace empowers humans to respond to God's revelation, making faith not just a human decision but a divinely-enabled trust that relies entirely on God's mercy.

Chapter 8: Faith in Practice: The Transformational Power of Trust

Q1: How does faith transform a believer's life?

A1: Faith shapes the believer's values, decisions, and actions, producing trust, obedience, and reliance on God even in challenging circumstances.

Q2: How can Christians nurture faith in their daily lives?

A2: Faith grows through spiritual disciplines such as prayer, meditation on scripture, and fellowship, which deepen trust and reliance on God.

Chapter 9: Faith, Works, and Belief: Clarifying Misconceptions

Q1: How does James 2 clarify the relationship between faith and works?

A1: James explains that faith is shown by works; true faith naturally leads to actions aligned with God's will, demonstrating that faith and works are inseparable.

Q2: Why is it incorrect to think of faith and works as separate?

A2: Faith and works are two parts of a single process; belief transforms into faith, which then produces works as an outward evidence of a transformed life.

Chapter 10: Faith and Salvation: A Gift Beyond Belief

Q1: How does Ephesians 2:8-9 explain salvation through faith?

A1: Salvation is by grace through faith, not by human effort. This faith is a divine gift that brings salvation into reality through a transformative relationship with God.

Q2: What is the role of belief and faith in salvation?

A2: Belief is necessary to accept the truth of the gospel, but faith goes further, embracing and committing to God's salvation, resulting in a transformed heart and life.

Chapter 11: Nurturing Faith Beyond Belief

Q1: What are some practical ways to nurture faith?

A1: Faith can be nurtured through prayer, studying scripture, participating in a faith community, and practicing spiritual disciplines that deepen trust in God.

Q2: Why is it important to go beyond mere belief in nurturing faith?

A2: While belief accepts God's truths, faith requires growth in trust and action, transforming belief into an enduring, committed relationship with God.

Chapter 12: Conclusion: Living in Faith, Beyond Belief

Q1: What is the practical significance of distinguishing between faith and belief?

A1: Distinguishing between them helps believers to move beyond intellectual acceptance of truth into a committed, trusting relationship with God that manifests in every area of life.

Q2: How does faith sustain a Christian's relationship with God beyond belief?

A2: Faith involves a living trust that shapes attitudes, decisions, and actions, enabling Christians to live confidently in God's promises and purpose, regardless of life's challenges.

These questions and answers will reinforce each chapter's key points, helping readers to reflect deeply on the concepts and apply them in their faith journey.